Remembering Who You Really Are

Remembering Who You Really Are

The Journey of Awakening to Soul

Ronda Ackles LaRue, M.S.

Foreword by Richard Moss, M.D.

iUniverse, Inc.
New York Lincoln Shanghai

Remembering Who You Really Are
The Journey of Awakening to Soul

iUniverse, Inc.

For information address:
iUniverse, Inc.
2021 Pine Lake Road, Suite 100
Lincoln, NE 68512
www.iuniverse.com

ISBN: 0-595-29158-9

Printed in the United States of America

"…Approach it and there is no beginning;
follow it and there is no end.
You can't know it, but you can be it,
at ease in your own life,
Just realize where you come from:
this is the essence of wisdom."

—*Tao Te Ching,* Stephen Mitchell

New English Version,©1988
Harper/Perennial Edition, 1991, p.14
Harper Collins Publishers, New York, NY

Contents

Foreword

by Richard Moss, M.D.

What you are about to read is a wonderfully honest, lyrically written, and profoundly insightful discussion of the most essential of all human endeavors, the journey to know oneself. For me there is no question that this is the fundamental purpose of a human life. I have spent more than three decades addressing human suffering with thousands of people and I have found that whether the suffering is caused by illness, unfortunate circumstances, or the most common, severe and persistent of all human suffering—that which we inflict upon ourselves and each other in our relationships—there is only one true remedy: remembering who we really are. This is simply so: not money, nor science, nor religion, nor politics, can do any more than institutionalize our ignorance until we can stand up in our lives and live from real faith in our true essence. Then everything else falls into place and we unshakably know what really matters, or at least what does not deserve our allegiance, and we begin to live authentically with hearts that can truly love.

One of the privileges of my lifework is that it enables me to meet fascinating people, people perhaps like yourself who are asking the important questions: Who am I? Why am I here? It was through my work that I met Ronda Larue. She had read my books, and eventually approached me when she felt the need for a particular kind of soul mirroring. She discusses this here and her perspective on how to choose and engage a teacher is very intelligently stated. For me, our association has been a rich, at times challenging, but thoroughly enjoyable one, one in which I feel I have received certainly as much as I was able to offer. Thus, it is with great pleasure that I now take this opportunity to introduce Ronda's first book to you.

It has been said that, "many are called, but few are chosen." One of the greatest mysteries is that of an individual's readiness to respond to the call of the soul. Why do so many of us go through our lives victims of our conditioning, when it is clear to see how deadening and destructive this often is? Why would we live without responding to our soul's "still, small voice", its gentle but insistent call to self-transcendence? The answer I believe is fear. We distrust the possibility of a life of fullness; we haven't suffered enough, I guess.

If you are thumbing through this book, you are undoubtedly among those fortunate ones who have suffered enough and whose soul has called you to face some of those fears and examine your life anew. As such you are on the way already to becoming more than you now know yourself to be. My guess is that it is your deep resonance with spirit—that which has brought tears of recognition to your eyes—which has made you want more and be ready for more in your life.

What *Remembering Who You Really Are* will help you to more fully grasp, is what it means to choose to answer that call. It will be an especially helpful companion through the inevitable dark time when we each must grope our way blindly, literally learning a new language of being. As Ronda writes, "As long as we keep looking for clues and answers and solutions to life's questions in the same logic stream of our accustomed linear mental functions, we're doomed to missing God's voice."

To discover the mysterious language in which our souls speak to us, we must first begin to deconstruct the illusion of who we have come to believe we are and allow ourselves to arrive at unknowing. Said in another way, we will run into ourselves and fall on our faces again and again until we finally learn to let go and trust what is. In speaking of this surrender process, Ronda comments, "stepping down from that with which we are identified without ever being able to 'know' (in the conventional sense) much less control, that which simply arises as spontaneous creation—is the foundation on which the awakening journey rests."

Ronda says that she intentionally chose to write a vulnerable exposé that reveals the journey itself, but what she also does so brilliantly is discuss the universal principles of such a journey. In this way, it becomes all of our journeys. Perhaps this is why I found the book so inductive. What she does so well here is to describe the journey in language that does not mire us down in old ways of thinking about enlightenment as some final state, or in images long ago co-opted by conventional religion. Her language is fresh, sometimes shockingly so. With saucy irony, she is humorously "in our faces", always talking right to us, always intimately challenging and inviting us to live with her through a process that eventually calls her beyond hope, as all deeper questing invariably will, until what we have been seeking is revealed to have been with us all along. We just didn't have the eyes to see.

I know from my own life that when someone makes the effort to write of their journey to reality, they are already addressing an audience of others who are similarly being called and whose paths can be, if not unburdened, at least made more direct. *Remembering Who You Really Are* charts the journey well, especially because this book is about the nitty-gritty of awakening by a woman who has carved her own path through an eclectic, non-traditional approach and tells it like it is. For example, I love it when Ronda writes, "The truth of who we really are is not found in the sensational, nor is it achieved though *dead*-ication to the mastery of a spiritual practice." In my observation, too many spiritual teachings emphasize a practice, until the practice becomes "the way" and self-realization becomes confused with the states of awareness such practices tend to cultivate. Meanwhile, as Ronda shows, the real work is anything but sensational. I believe women intrinsically respect nitty-gritty; they have spent millennia persecuted, disenfranchised, but always expected to pick up the pieces. As I look out at the world of "spirituality", it is still too much a man's world, articulated in a manner more accommodating to how men are enculturated and where women who follow these paths risk burying something of an innate feminine wisdom. That wisdom fills the pages of this book, to the benefit of all of us.

This book does not make any effort at ennobling or romanticizing the journey. It does not offer the mystique of a special spiritual practice, nor does it make promises that seduce egos. This book is going to fall into your hands because you are ready and probably have felt confused and maybe at times demoralized by so much of what has been presented to you as the "spiritual" path. I think everyone, men and women alike, have had this feeling about their journey at times, that it loses its compelling realness when it becomes part of what the consensus spiritual world seems to be saying such a journey is about and *how* it should be taken. In refreshing contrast, what you will find in these pages is an authentic story of spiritual emergence, not identical to yours, but with very rich insight and no effort to coerce your belief. It is a living testimony of the awakening process that is always a spontaneously creative discovery that must be lived uniquely by each of us.

Remembering Who You Really Are is a welcome draught of intelligence, humility, and enthusiasm for life, and stands as far as I am concerned in the timeless lineage of mystical accounts that express the soul's seeking to free itself from the encumbrances of enculturation so that it can sing its song with renewed and impudent aliveness.

Richard Moss
Oakhurst, California

Introduction

o o o o o o o o o o o o o o o o o o o o o o o o o o o o o o o o o o o

"…only the paradox comes anywhere near to comprehending the fullness of life."

—C.G. Jung, *Psychology And Alchemy*

A little over a year ago something terrible and marvelous happened to me: I became nobody. Wasn't planning on it. Didn't expect it. Everything just stopped: my professional research consulting business of 18 years, my art work, social interactions, service in the community, even phone calls (except the relentless telemarketers—nothing will stop them!)

I say I didn't want or expect this, and that is true. I did however pray to know my soul's intent. As the saying goes:

"Be careful what you ask for…"

I prayed very intently a couple of years ago to be led to understand the deep meaning of life. I issued (what I call) a *living prayer*—a prayer arising from the depths of one's soul. I stated unequivocally that I found no purpose to live other than in service to the spiritual journey. My living prayer must have been a good one. It reverberated into the vast Eternal Dreaming—and spun back, hurtling me into the cave of my undoing. It was here I began in earnest my life-long apprenticeship with the mystic.

"In the beginning was the Word…"

◆   ◆   ◆

All my life, I, like many (if not each one) of us, have felt a deep yearning—a kind of romantic pining and search to find this, this *something*, that I could somehow feel and yet that remained ever just outside of my reach. At times it felt like

1

something I could almost taste on my tongue, a savory flavor I could not quite identify. I often felt as if I were trying to find something I had lost; trying to remember something I'd forgotten. I was looking for something, but I could not quite see what it was. I suspect you have felt this too.

This book is for those who sense that there is something essential stirring within the current of everyday living, something of deep purpose asking to be noticed and claimed. There is.

It feels like the desire for love, a longing for abiding joy and peace. But it is more than that, and it *is* that too. This deep inner yearning for happiness, wholeness, and fulfillment is the calling of your true nature. It is the sacred age-old call to take up the quest, to enter the Journey to Soul, to Remember...

There is a voice calling out to each of us. It is calling all the time through the passageways of our normal everyday living; calling us to look and listen more deeply, inviting us to come home within the fullness of our original Being. It whispers through the heart of our desiring; it calls through the sound of our worries and confusion; it cries out through the devastation of a life crisis—ushering us to the entrance of the *invisible doorway of awakening* by way of our questioning:

"What is my life's purpose?"
"What is the meaning behind my struggles?"
"Why am I here?"

This voice within our hearts we call by many names: God, Source, Divine Intelligence, Beloved. Some call the personalized aspect of this, the "still small voice", Soul, Original Self, our True Nature. All our words are ultimately unsuitable. Each objectifies that which is before any reference. Each places a name on that which is forever nameless and before the "naming". But name we must. I've come to referent God or Source as the *Great Eternal Dreaming* because it implies something of the mysteriously moving and endlessly creating intelligence in which we ourselves move, breathe, and have our being.

I use the word *Remembering* over words like "awakening", because it implies an ongoing, ceaseless activity of re-uniting (re-*membering*) within the fullness of *who* we are. I still do use other words for remembering, as I do the various words for God, for soul, ego, etc. because I realize we all have different stings and stereotypes as well as common understandings, and so the fluid and alternating use of various words and their substitutes is necessary in my attempt to convey meaning across as wide a canvas as possible. Same holds true for the use of he, she, one, it. There's no good solution. I simply alternate and hope you can hear one if you cannot the other.

◆   ◆   ◆

This calling to remember *who we really are* is the primary and sacred calling of Life—the reason we are here. It is the unfolding of our Soul, the realization of our *primary beingness*, the ultimate experience and expression of living. It is *the One* ever knowing Itself through *the many*. It is *the many* coming to know themselves within *the One*.... The Lover reaching out to be embraced in the arms of the Beloved, formlessness being kissed by form, the void falling in love with time and space.

The great sacred texts of the world's religions choose different words to express this embrace, this fundamental and conscious re-membering of Soul and Source. They speak of one becoming "enlightened", "Self-realized", "awakened", or "born again", to describe one who has experienced a radical transformation of being, the presence of the Holy Spirit, or the hand of Grace.

Words are a problem: utterly misleading. I hesitate (cringe a little even) to use words like "enlightened" and "awakened". They have become so objectified with over/and misuse that they have started to become looked upon as "places"—and then we fall into one of the biggest pitfalls on the path: thinking that there is a state "enlightened" that one can *achieve* and then *"ah, journey's done, I've arrived, I've become enlightened!"* as if we can *"go out and get us one"* like we do a new car, placing it out in front for all to see. Isn't this exactly how many who claim enlightenment seem to treat it? Truly, this is one of, if not *the* biggest false god we make from a fundamental misunderstanding by way of transcribing our standard paradigm of identification onto something that requires a complete letting go.

The truth of who we are is not found in the sensational nor is it *achieved* through *dead*-ication to the mastery of a spiritual practice.

Our highest purpose and our Original Self can only become truly discovered and fully expressed right here, in the ordinary acts of living—in the simple meat and juice of life—in the daily embodiment of conscious Presence. Your Soul's purpose is forever proclaimed here in this moment—it is vibrantly announced in your questions, your struggles, your desires. Only a thin veil separates the ending of your search within the realization of an *a priori* wholeness...

◆   ◆   ◆

This is a book about coming to the end of the spiritual search. But oddly and paradoxically, coming to the end of the spiritual search requires a journey, a hero's journey into the mythic landscape of forgetting and re-membering *who we really are*. Like the epic film *The Wizard of Oz,* it is a journey into finding the Fullness of Being through an integration of heart, mind, and will. And like Dorothy, when her journey is complete, we quite simply return and see home with new eyes. The journey reclaims us within the musical language of the Complete. The end of the spiritual search is the beginning of living within each new moment—it is a dying into Life, a falling into Love.

I offer this book as a contemporary voice for finding one's way along the age-old path of remembering. I have tried to give you that which would have most helped me at a time when I was in the midst of a spiritual life-crisis, and blinded to the inner awakening it was ever offering me.

In much of this book I share openly with you the personal experience of my own remembering: how I initiated it, what transpired, and what I saw and learned along the way. It is a travelogue into the universal journey of Soul through the story of my own awakening experience. At times it is very personal and raw. These are very personal and very raw places. I want to illuminate the dark crevasses, and not just the transcendent grace or "intellectual wisdom" of this awakening movement in consciousness.

Awakening is *not* about transcendence. It is not about a showy wisdom that leads others to believe that's where this journey leads one to rest. (There is no resting "place".) I show my own rawness because I want there to be no mistake: "Being awakened" is not a place! It is not a place.

The awakening experience is an ushering into a forever-moving moment of remembering. To "be awakened" is not a place, but a fundamental and ceaseless process of consecrating one's life to radical reformation within the presence of Being.

The amazing grace is not being "saved", as in achieving transcendent enlightenment. The true amazing grace, and the great miracle, is awakening to the continual flow of remembering that is forever available within each moment through the presence of one's attention. It is a continual surrendering of the illusions of self-identification in an unconditional free-fall into the arms of life—not once and for all, but as a continual renewal and re-uniting—God seeing Itself in each moment of remembering.

...It is becoming a more attentive partner in the stunningly magnificent and endless dance of the lover for the Beloved.

◆   ◆   ◆

The call to awakening is a call to an entirely different language, to an entirely different way of experiencing than we have become accustomed. (It is even more obscure than learning a new language—more like if you were to learn to hear and to communicate in the language of a tree, and even that's relatively simpler.) We are called to step closer to the musical language and rhythm of unity, not a unity that excludes the parts, but a unity that encompasses even multiplicity. It is language fundamentally foreign to our linear and dualistic ways of thinking and being.

In my past I have tended toward the academic, typically leaning toward intellectual and logical arguments and "scientific proofs". In my graduate training as a research scientist I was quite versed in references, quotes, statistics, naming names. Smart, indisputable, impressive these academic ways; but I've been gentled. I've come to know a language that is much more deeply penetrating, beautiful, and real. It is closer to the Heart.

To train the ears and eyes for realizing an entirely different kind of language requires that we *let go* the ways we currently listen, hear and think. I pray that the musical lilt of the living language of Unity will sing through these words. I hope you can listen in a different way, with "soft ears" and a quieting of the mind.

Have you ever read a book in which you realized that more is being said than "what is being said"? Like that, let what is living between and around the words slip in and surprise you. It is from an engaged state of empty receptivity that the musical language of unity slips in. Again the paradox: "engaged" (an act of volition) and "empty receptivity" (passive, without a driving agenda). Let spring from inside of you, your own inner resonance and remembrance of this rounded musical language of *All That Is*.

◆   ◆   ◆

So, here is the journey of remembering. Here, with my prayer, is a light shining along the trail of the story of why we are here. It is a trail that leads through odd twists and turns, coming at last to the remembering of who you really are and always have been.

The book is organized into three main sections. Part I presents the key ideas and elements in awakening to *who we really are*. It is not just a matter of "be here now" and "*Voila! I'm alive in the moment!*" There is something that first needs to be seen, undone, and surrendered. This first section is a kind of prologue of the ground to come. It is like a blanket set out at the trailhead to the Journey of Soul, where you may sit, contemplate the journey, pull together a few supplies, stretch your legs.

Part II is an account of the awakening process. In this section I share my personal encounters and experiences during the descent of my undoing, and the reformation of my being as grounded in remembering who *I Am*. This section shows by way of travelogue, the common terrain and pitfalls encountered on this sacred journey. Here you can put your head on the pillow of my storytelling, and be ushered into the sacred land of awakening. In my experience, there is valuable insight that may be gained by hearing and contemplating a frank exposé of the awaking process that simply cannot be transmitted any other way except one's own deep journey (and that's next).

In Part III, I summarize what I have found to be the keys to initiating and traversing the mystic's quest. While my friends and family know me to be inherently anti-technique and disdainful of "how to's" of almost any sort, I discovered for myself in my own journey into the mystic, some basic inner truths about this process of re-membering who we really are. There are a couple of keys that are especially helpful in some of the confusing dark places as well as some of the glorious ones. Rather than being tools *per se*, they are more like a conceptual map offering an orientation for keeping in sight the expression of faith and the claiming of your own sacred story.

◆   ◆   ◆

There is a dance we're called to make. It is a spectacular opening into something much larger than the mechanisms of the mind can embrace, and yet it is something that we intuitively know: it is *who* we really are. It is the very ground in which we all move, breathe, and have our being.

We are each (you and I) a fantastically unique spectrum of consciousness with incredible and unique talents, gifts, and temperaments, *and* we are also more than that: we are Consciousness ever more aware of Itself. We are an integral part of what I call the *Eternal Dreaming* in a *Great and Godly Game of Hide and Seek*…forever separating and uniting, forgetting and remembering.

And, my God, what a mysteriously beautiful and awesome dance!

So, come to this, my storytelling of the Remembering, and let it be a flame igniting the telling of yours. And so by each story told, will another one remember, and thus the Great Dreaming awakes.

Ronda Ackles LaRue
Ojai, California

PART I
Forgetting…

1

Into the Mystic

"We were born before the wind
Also younger than the sun..."

—Van Morrison, Into the Mystic

As far back as I can remember I've been keenly curious about matters of God, truth, the meaning of life. I remember, like many of us perhaps do, gazing at the stars as a young child, trying to understand infinity.

Growing up in a deeply spiritual home, the idea of God caught my attention very early. My parents explained God to me, my brothers and sisters, as *Infinite Intelligence*. I used to ask my mom, as part of the endless and exhausting *"why"* stage of development, many questions about God and infinity: *"How can there be such a thing as infinity? What created infinity? How can there be no beginning and no end?"* In truth, I am still in awe of these questions.

All my life I have lived with a driving desire to know truth; to understand why we are here; to understand the meaning of life. I've been an avid reader in areas of cultural beliefs and religion, spirituality, transformation, social psychology, and the evolution of consciousness. The magnificent mystery amazes and charms me with a desire to open the box and find out what's inside, and to step out and find what's beyond.

I grew up a child in love with nature. I spent hours alone outdoors, idly picking up sticks and stones, making of them small altars to life left here and there along my wanderings. I've always felt a bit more like a wood imp than human, most happy alone out of doors or lying around with my dogs under a tree. Long before I knew the word ritual, I would quite naturally make up ceremonies and perform them as a celebratory communion with God stirring through me and all of life. So awesome, nature! My home today is more outdoors than in, by way of the bits and pieces of leaf and twig hanging on walls and set out on tables. And, if the truth be told, I prefer to pee behind bushes and trees than in some glazed, powder blue toilet. I really do, as my friends will attest (some in dismay, others with an odd regard).

I am blessed with a natural inclination toward a celebration of life. I enjoy its odd twists and turns, the geometry that spins out of chaos, the strangely perfect paradox. Amazing all. There is a profound relationship to life that comes from sacred communion, something I believe we're all born knowing but that most of us forget (or have had trained out of us).

Thanks to my mother, an amazingly playful and soulful being of rare spirited aliveness, I never lost this innate communion with life. As I was growing up, she reinforced by example the essence of unconditional love, grace, and childlike worship. It took me half a lifetime to realize how truly rare is such a precious gift. She always delighted in the uniqueness of each of us. As such, we were each individually honored as unique reflections of God.

> …I wonder: what would change in our world if each of the babies born on just this one day were given such a gift—the gift of keeping the knowledge of her own deep Self?…

By career, my father was an engineer/executive and my mother an artist. Hence I grew up both scientifically-oriented and artistically-blessed. As children we were encouraged by Dad to stretch our abilities into various pursuits of athletic, cultural, and mechanical accomplishment regardless of gender or politic, and to do it with integrity, competence, and self-sufficiency. I bought his "*If you want something done right, do it yourself*" hook, line and sinker. It became my living mantra. With Mom, we were encouraged to express freely our artistic and playful natures—whether painting on the floors or pulling impish pranks on one another in good fun. She had our hands in art before we could talk, and I began sculpting in clay at the age of three with my first series: *Snow Storm*. (Well, that's what those blops were to me.)

Art to me is spontaneous playfulness, co-creation, and worship with the elements of life, and it is my deep abiding passion. It is holy ground for me. And so art became my sacred occupation, and I went on to prepare for "the real world" studying business, psychology, and sociology. My undergraduate degree was a three-way major leading to a master's of science degree from the school of sociology in (get this title): *Applied Social Research and Evaluation Methodology* (gotta love academia, the long-windedness alone!).

Growing up (and even more recently than I care to admit as an adult) I was pretty proud of my self-sufficient, self-righteous, quick-witted, and opinionated self. I wore it like a badge protecting my deeper, softer heart. Was a time I would "fight with the best of them"—and win...or die trying. (It's part of that *oldest sibling thing* that we eldest set up to maintain the pecking order—i.e., *"don't get mad, get (more than) even!")* This served me well in the corporate world where, if done right, it is highly respected and rewarded. It doesn't do diddly-squat in the artistic community, but that's another story.

In short, I lived most of my early and mid-adulthood as one who proudly "didn't need anyone" and who ran circles around anyone who tried to get in. *"I'll do it myself"* was my mainstay. I was self-sufficient and self-assured, even in my spiritual quest. The idea of teachers and "how to" books were for lost seekers, and I surely wasn't that. Nope, pretty self-contained and confident was I.

My life was not (and is not now) all "bliss". Having grown up in a large, boisterous family in the 1960's with solid Presbyterian, farmland values transposed onto a Chicago suburban 60's radical culture, I also got into my share of "Trouble with a capital T". And I've made more than my share of misguided decisions, loss of vision, diversions and distractions of all sorts. Oh, all of it, you know: affairs, and hopeless loves; over-indulgence and addiction to pleasure; self-absorption in my own trivialities. As the saying goes: *"sex and rock 'n roll."* I was a "Cadillac squeezed into a VW frame", as a former lover used to say. I had so much energy that I ran full speed and reckless on an inevitable collision course with my heart...

Through all these growing up mishaps and the pitfalls of becoming lost in the various identities I created, I've nonetheless always maintained an avid interest and vast reading appetite for matters of spirituality, evolution, physics, and metaphysics. Even through my many years of self-sufficient diversions and distractions, I can see (upon looking back) that they were simply poorly-directed (and perhaps necessary) attempts to meet my soul. Like so many of us, and as reflected in the old Waylon Jennings country song, I was *"looking for love in all the wrong places."* Yet through it all, the unique voice of my Soul's calling was always here in the background, patient and ever leading me closer to the heart of my true self.

I believe this is so for each of us. I believe there is an ever-patient calling, and sooner or later (whether it is this year or five lifetimes from now) the voice of your own Soul will bring you to Life's full embrace. Even when we're (seemingly) off the path, somewhere deep down we're each being called to the Re-membering.

◆   ◆   ◆

"How shall we know our purpose in life? How can we live our highest calling? How do we heal our wounds? How will we redeem ourselves?" These are some of the questions arising from an inner calling to remember who we really are. And we struggle and search and seek in all sorts of ways to find answers; to find solace and relief from this inner nagging call. We look to experts, teachers, churches, "how-to" books, therapies, pills. We're not looking in the wrong places so much as with the wrong expectations, the wrong paradigm, the wrong basic orientation: to find answers, to find relief, to be at peace.

"What is a life well lived? How alive to Life do you dare be in the moment of now, and now, and again now?" These questions *are* the awakening. These questions (not their answers) *are* the enlightenment to the potential within each moment of being born anew. These questions are the very consecration of your awareness to the story of your soul's journey as it unfolds in living presence.

It is a matter of this: *"To what do you point your compass of awareness within this moment? How attentive to your soul's journey are you willing to be?"*

This is the *One Story:* The story of Soul's purpose.

We're each called to this one story regardless of profession, race, income, family structure, or religious beliefs. I call this the "Journey to Soul", or our *original prayer:* Life calling you, me, each of us to the remembering of *who we really are.* The seeming riddles of life are answered within each one's story of unfolding presence. We each are called to the one great story of remembering. To live this story, it must be claimed. It must be acknowledged—attended to. The claiming *is* the awakening. Can you see that this is so? If not now, by the end of this book I hope you shall. It is your highest calling, the reason why you are here.

◆   ◆   ◆

The spotlight on my own awakening quest and the experiences I encountered, is the best way I have discovered to illuminate the pathway of your own remembering. It is the telling of the one universal story through the sharing of my own awakening journey. The deepest universal truths are embedded and alive within the act of the storytelling. This has always been so. This is the story we are each called to claim. I tell of my journey simply so that you may better recognize and tell yours.

I want to give you all of it, not just the bright revelations, but the down and dirty struggle, confusion, and ceaseless questioning. I want to give you all things alive and squirming. Only dead words put things in neat boxes, structures, and belief systems. I want these words to breathe and sigh, cry out and be very very still—the kind of stillness where all infinite potential spills over. This is where the awakening is: here, now, just like that!

It is through exposing the personal vulnerability of my own journey—"the good, the bad, and the ugly"—that I hope to reveal the elusive passageway into the musical language of awakening. It is in the language of paradox that we find the voice of Creation. It is a difficult language for us to hear. And yet, it is so elegantly simple and forever right here.

Enlightenment is not "a place" but rather an attunement of our listening abilities to the musical language of unity that surrounds and envelops us. Like white noise, we no longer hear what is forever all around us. We must become supple to a language of paradox, something our dualistic and linear minds find impossible to understand, and very difficult to embrace. Therein lies the key.

It is the fluidity of living within paradox that *is* the awakening—not finding peace of mind, not coming to rest in an assurance of truth, not finding answers to the questions as we've posed them.

We ask the wrong questions, and they must eventually be seen through and given up. This is why a fluidity with paradox is so essential on this path.

All the mystical writings throughout the ages and across all main religions speak in their own way to this journey of remembering. It is what Joseph Campbell calls the "Hero's Journey"; it is an epic tale of peril that demands a steadfastness of purpose. It is the journey to finding and reclaiming one's birthright. It is the proclaiming of one's purpose in life. It is the claiming of one's true destiny. It is how we come to know the truth of our selves, how our deepest potential becomes realized in service to Life, how our destiny is lived. And it is a journey of great difficulty; a journey that demands the calling forth of one's deepest integrity, vigilance of self-awareness, and strength of character. This is the journey of becoming fully alive and living life fresh, in the moment of now. "...*The Kingdom of Heaven is within.*"

"*How do we come to know the Kingdom of Heaven? How do we come to know the Truth of our Self? How do we come to live in the fullness of Being?*" Many speak of the necessity of a fundamental "undoing" of all one's presently held structures of identity that precedes a radical reorganization into the fullness of Being. Inevitable to this process is meeting the *darkness of unknowing* and the *fear of non-being*, what St. John of the Cross called "the dark night of the soul". It is through the process of meeting and facing (not backing away from) the dark night of the soul, that we find the secret miracle of an eternal inner light. And in that very facing, comes the fundamental revelation: it is through a process of continual surrendering to *what is*, that we are continually born anew. (I am reminded here of something that gifted teacher/author Byron Katie (*The Work*™; wwwthework.com) often recites: "*When you argue with reality, you lose—but only one hundred percent of the time.*"

◆   ◆   ◆

The journey of awakening to one's authenticity, is a journey of surrender. *Ooop!* I know! Few are comfortable with that word. The word *surrender* has got a bad rap. It's a pill that doesn't go down too well for most of us. But it is so of awakening. Awakening is coming to know one's Source through a continual process of surrender into *unknowing*; it is a conscious laying down of the habitual ways we respond in an attempt to maintain control and protect the belief of our "separateness". We must surrender these conditioned automatic responses so that we may live here, now, in direct authentic relationship with Life as it moves through you and me. Surrendering is a movement in worship (what I call a *living prayer*) inspired by a deep yearning for the re-*membering* of our Oneness.

This doesn't mean we give up our personalities or our personal character. It's not a matter of killing the personal ego to become a "*sweet Omming bundle of boundless love*". It is precisely this kind of black or white dualistic thinking (*it's gotta be one or the other*) that keeps so many of us lost and struggling on the wrong quest for years, if not lifetimes. This either/or thinking reflects a fundamental error in understanding the awakening call. (Actually, it is more than that; it is a fundamental lack of true surrender, too.)

This is not an easy journey. It's fraught with unpredictable twists and turns, diversions and distractions. There are things (monsters and other creepy things) in disguise, hiding in wait. Things shape-shift and disappear only to pop up somewhere new and unexpected. Things aren't what they seem. All the usual tools don't work worth a damn; they are useless (in the way, in fact).

We're constantly dogged by illusion and fear, all the more powerful and difficult to see through because they are of our own construction, the very fabric we've used to create the box we don't realize we're in. Tricky business, this! Way beyond the capabilities of the mind—and, the idea that there is something beyond the capabilities of the mind is so completely absurd (and threatening) to our ever-chattering and clever mind, it creates all sorts of pitfalls, diversions, and trick mirrors to obscure the path and to maintain the lofty position to which it has ascribed itself. Truly this mystic's journey is one of epic proportion. It requires a full surrender into non-being and a free-fall into unknowing. Maybe the soul wants this, but the mind absolutely does not…no way. Uh-uh!

A steady intent, a true *living prayer*—and Grace—are one's only hope on this path.

Poem/Prayer: The Calling

(Part I. I Await You)

I await you
Oh Ceaseless Stirring,
Oh Infinite Creating;
Wave upon wave with no stop and no start.

I sit silent
And await your coming (as surely you must)
Like the coastal fog up our canyon;
A marking of entrance to nightfall.
The cadence of Time's lonely breath.

Like some slow moving sea dragon
You come
At my bidding,
Intent to devour me whole.

You circle and undulate around my closed lids,
A sea of blue dreams seeking form.

Delicate and delicious, patient and yet palpable;
No hurry to lift the veil.
No hurry. No rush at all.

My fate has already been spoken.
The serpent already caught its tail.
That which is seeking, is that being sought
In this ancient and ritual dance:

> The Lover and her Beloved,
> So sweetly entwined.

> Ah forever, we're held like this
> In an endless Eternal Great Breathing!...

2

The Great and Godly Game of Hide and Seek

Why is it we all seem to struggle so? Why so much dissatisfaction? We never seem quite satisfied with who we are, with what life brings, with where we are in ourselves. It's almost as if, were we satisfied, we fear there'd be no more reason for us to live; as if the Creator might descend on some big burst of light and pluck us straight away:

"This one's done! Beam him up, Scotty."

I've had that bizarre fear myself, the fear that if I allow myself to feel satisfied, happy even, well then, the (presupposed) fall will be so much worse. Safer to stay slightly *under*, slightly under-fulfilled. That way I can protect myself from some lurking devastation; slip in under the radar. It's as if, by giving myself an intermittent fix of unease, I'll never have to suffer one of the "really big ones"...*Stay closer to down and the bottom won't hurt so bad.* (Something like that.) Stupid of course. Still, many of us do this through much of our lives, I've noticed.

Do we all live with some inherent fear of unworthiness? Is there something in the process of birth and the slow differentiation of self that leaves us each carrying a basic wound, no matter how loving and nurturing the home?

Is there something in the *Fall from Grace* itself that is forever imprinted on each Soul; something in being cast from the *Garden* that jump-starts the inner yearning for our slow return?

Is this internal stir of dissatisfaction, Life's built-in wake up call?

I think this is so.

◆   ◆   ◆

God (Creation, or if you prefer, the Ground of Being) wanting to know and experience itself, requires reflection—requires *the Fall* into differentiation and form in order to have reference to itself. Without this separation into differentiated form, there is no discernment—no "knowing"—and therefore no dynamic of "the observer observing the observed". Without this dynamic, all would remain formless, undifferentiated consciousness. God, Source, could not step out of Itself to see and know Itself.

And so, here we are, in a ceaseless dynamic interplay of Allness within differentiation, a great cosmic breathing: re-membering Unity, and *Fall-ing* back into duality and the timeline of subject/object reference.

What frolic, this never-ending yearning to separate and to unite! I call it the *Great and Godly Game of Hide and Seek.* And we're, each of us, an integral part of this Godly Frolic.

Dissatisfaction was built into the equation (hard-wired into our very cells) if only to perpetuate the movement to hide and to seek. Life itself, stirred by its own aliveness:

"*Move!*" Life continually calls out…"*This isn't it.*" the psyche hears.

This is one oddly conceived game. The one hiding is seeking. The one seeking is in hiding, in a game that never finishes. No winners, no losers (though we keep believing ourselves one or the other in alternating fame). No pushing the clock forward to hurry things along, though we pretend that we can, are, and have.… *Ahh* to feel as one of the Enlightened few…

Somewhere *out there* the Referee must have thrown up his hands. (…Somewhere right here too!) I want to say: "*So let's all just loosen up. Let's be good sports.*"

In the game of hide and seek, at some point in the game, the Seeker yells out, "*Ally, ally, in free. Come out, come out, wherever you are!*"

…And all those who are hidden, come join around the Tree of Life.

◆   ◆   ◆

Most of us don't think we're lost from ourselves. Oh, we may feel that inner stir of "dissatisfaction"; that itching sense of never quite feeling at peace, never being quite whole, a sense that something is missing. And we seek all sorts of ways, from comic to tragic, to scratch the itch of dissatisfaction.

Most often we seek to pinpoint the cause of these feelings of dissatisfaction in the circumstances of our present life: a wrong partner, the wrong career, definitely the wrong body! Or, we find the cause in our past: an abusive or neglectful parent, hurtful past relationships, wounds of all sorts. We spend countless hours pouring over these various causes to which we've attributed our feelings of dissatisfaction. We spend thousands of dollars on therapies, groups, pills, and countless other modalities that promise to heal the causes of our dissatisfactions and dis-ease.

We try new partners, new jobs, jazzercise, cosmetic surgery, psychic readings, Stairmaster, church groups, pot, parties, books, a new SUV, yoga, yell therapy, wardrobe consultants, Feng Shui, meditation, affairs, and fantasies. An endless array, best I can see, hoping to *fix* ourselves of this nagging inner feeling of dissatisfaction. It seems we're ever in a state of "not quite right". In fact, most of us have many "not quite rights" going on all the time. Interesting, don't you think, this basic dissatisfaction, and the constant efforting to fix it?

It seems quite clear to me that we live in a continual circularity: trying to fix "not quite right", but none of these *fix-its* stop the itch. It may solve one problem. We just go on the next one stacked up in a line—and then another and another. Why is that, do you suppose?

I wonder if another perspective is required. I wonder if we're looking at "the problem" from too close in. I wonder if we're looking inside of the box for the troubles and not at the box itself.

Earlier, I spotlighted this intrinsic feeling of dissatisfaction as a built-in part of what I call the *Great and Godly Game of Hide and Seek*; i.e., I spoke of dissatisfaction as an intrinsic calling from Life into the never-ending game of separation and unity, forgetting and remembering. From this perspective, what we feel inside as "not quite right" is that yearning by God-in-us to re-unite and to re-member. But to unite and to remember, we also have to continually separate and forget. Otherwise, we fall back into undifferentiated consciousness and there is no more knowing. So we forget, and re-member, forget, and re-member. The endless great breathing of God…

Let me say this another way: The very nature of separation of Source into form in order to express and to know Itself implies that we inherently live within the cycle of dissatisfaction. It is so by the nature of the dynamic interplay between unity and separation: God knowing, seeing, and expressing Itself through us. There has to be a tension to re-member, and a tension to separate and forget so that there can be the call back to remembering: perfect cyclical tension sparking each next breath, in the endless breathing of God in us.

"OK", I hear you say.
"So we're stuck with dissatisfaction. What do I do with that?"

Good question…

◆   ◆   ◆

For me, realizing the role of dissatisfaction as inherent to the process of God (Consciousness) knowing Itself through us (as individuation) takes us out of the box. It relieves us from the burden of trying to *fix* ourselves through all the myriad modifications of circumstance that we try, and opens us instead to the potential of an entirely new relationship to dissatisfaction: one that, rather than try and *fix it* (a.k.a. heal ourselves, change ourselves) sees dissatisfaction for what it is, sees it in the larger context of what it serves, and therefore moves with it as part of the flow of a vibrant living current.

This requires a fundamental change in perspective. No longer is the goal to *get rid of* the dissatisfaction in my life. No longer do I cling to the idea that there is something in myself or in my life that needs fixing, healing, changing. No longer is dissatisfaction considered the symptom of an underlying problem at all. Rather, I accept this thing we call and feel as "dissatisfaction" as a form of dynamic tension that is inherent to the Current of Life. I accept that it is part of the momentum that brings a separate "me" back into realization of Oneness: *"I Am That I Am."*

This perspective for me lives closer to truth. It is looking at life from a space that is bigger than the box of my own identity, my own separateness, or my own life circumstances. This perspective doesn't deny these things, it simply derives understanding and response from a larger viewpoint: one that embraces my separateness within a larger context of Oneness. It is a fundamental reorganization of being. It is the place mystics call realization, it is the realization of Life breathing me—and that

I Am the Breathing. It is coming to live within mystery and grace time and time again. It is a state of presence that denies no thing and acknowledges All.

This is the great paradox of Life. Truth abides all around us, and nowhere can it be found. Just as we can never quit the stirring of dissatisfaction that seduces each breath of separation and re-membering, we can never rest wholly in our Godliness nor wholly in our individualness. We can only come to see and to delight in this dance, the lover for the Beloved, as we fall into grace from time to time eternal.

SUGGESTED EXERCISE:
THE GAME OF HIDE AND SEEK

Create a space where you can lie down and be undisturbed for 20 minutes or so, and have nearby something with which you can write.

1.   Lying down in a comfortable position, take several very deep, relaxing breaths (breathing in as deeply as you can, and exhaling fully). Then for the next 10 minutes or so, continue to breathe deeply—not quite as full as you can, but as fully as you can and still be deeply relaxing. (You may choose to play some meditative music, but I suggest it be something that won't distract you from going inward.) As you begin to relax, sense into your Deepest Essence, into what you sense or hope or feel is your deepest potential or soul essence. It could come as a memory of a time when you felt very connected to life, or just as a sense of longing for that deepest part of yourself—your Soul.

2.   When you feel that you have touched a sense of your true essence, take a moment or two and then sit up and pull out your writing materials. Write out those times, places, and circumstances you feel most connected to your sense of soul: Where are/were you? What are you doing at those times? What do you feel inside when you are most connected to your soul? When was the last time you recall feeling this way?

3.   Then, and still from this sense of soul, start to notice all the ways (big or small) that you feel you hide from yourself: When and where are you least connected to your sense of soul? What are you doing at those times? What do you feel like? (Hint: look for times and ways that you are bored or depressed, anxious or irritable. Look for behaviors "you don't like" in yourself.)

4.   Next, list all the things you are dissatisfied with in your life. Things about yourself, things about your circumstances. (Some obvious places to start: your body image, your health, your career, your spouse, your sense of well-being—you get the idea.) Just put them all out on paper, as many as you can, saying, "I am dissatisfied with…." (We all have a "gazillion". Let it rip!)

5.   Now go back over the list of times, places, and ways in which you feel most connected to your soul. Try and just "feel into" that sense of soul. Offer a prayer to become more open to your soul's wisdom of expression in your life in whatever words or ways fit your expression right now.

6. Write this prayer (or the essence of it), with a mental note that you will observe how "dissatisfaction" continually comes into your life and how this dissatisfaction takes you away from or brings you toward soul. (You might wish to keep a journal, but don't over effort this part. It is better, in my experience, to let it be a gentle observation/contemplation kept in the back of your mind rather than something to try and "get right" or fully detailed.) Let your prayer to soul and your notice of dissatisfaction be gently with you over the next several days and weeks.

3

Getting Lost in Ourselves

○ ○
"...before I built a wall I'd ask to know what I was walling in or walling out...."

—Robert Frost, Mending Wall

We all get lost *from* our Self…We all get lost *in* our self. It happens naturally as a part of the process of becoming a separate functioning individual. It's part of the hide and seek game: God separating and hiding from Itself, in order to find and to delight Itself again and again in all of life.

Can you imagine the delight at each re-membering? *"Ah…here I am!"*

It's an interesting process, the way we hide from our Self. It has to do with being created in the image and likeness of God. We literally create our realities, then move into them, and forget that there is, or ever was, any other larger truth. We become a mini-universe of our own making.

In what I referred to in Chapter two as *the Great and Godly Game of Hide and Seek,* there are two major currents in this cycle of separating into form and re-uniting into One. There is the movement of forgetting (the movement of creating a separateness of identity), and there is the movement of re-membering (the movement of realizing and thereby reintegrating into wholeness or unity). It is a great, forever breathing in, and back out; universes unfolding and enfolding.

IDENTITY STRUCTURES: HOW WE BECOME LOST IN OURSELVES:

Each of us, when we're born, remains for quite some time in a relative state of undifferentiated consciousness. That is, we do not experience ourselves as separate from the environment around us. There is not yet the understanding of "me". (Impossible to fully appreciate this undifferentiated state, here now as a fully formed adult. It would blow our minds, literally.)

Slowly through the developmental process of individuation—that gradual development of a sense of self that emerges as we pass from the undifferentiated consciousness of infancy, into childhood identity, and later, into who we become as adults—each of us develops a personality (a set of patterned behaviors) in response to the unique circumstances of our genetics, our upbringing, and the culture in which we live. So, for example, I grew up to see myself as a white, middle-class, gutsy and independent, female artist, and social observer.... And you grew up seeing yourself as the various adjectives for experiences that form your unique makeup.

Quite soon we become identified with these personality characteristics, they become *who we are*, what separates *me* from *other*. These personality characteristics, or personas, become "me" and "you". They become the icons we use to distinguish ourselves from the field of *other* and *all*.

Once these personality structures have been constructed and put into place to support and declare who we are, most of us spend most of the rest of our days defending these personality structures, often as if our very lives depended upon it. And that's just what the ego-me and the ego-you believes true![1]

The ego, which stands to define and defend our identity in the world, serves an essential and invaluable function in life. Indeed, it is necessary to the early childhood formation of "I" as a functionally separate being. But as time goes on we get fooled: we start to think we *are* these self-manufactured identities, and we become trapped within these calcified response structures of our own making.

J. Krishmamurti, the world famous philosopher who lived much of his life in Ojai, California, and who gave talks in the oak grove very near where I live, dedicated virtually his entire lifetime in dialogue and inquiry into the nature of

---

1. *The "ego", as I'm using the term here, refers to that mechanism within each of us that seeks to establish and maintain our separate identity. I anthropomorphize the ego throughout much of this book for the sake of making a point. The ego as an entity that is separate from our self, clearly does not exist as such. But in speaking of it as if it were an entity, it makes it possible to "stand back" from its inherent and insidious means of operating in our lives, and look at it more objectively. Another more playful way to look at the ego is that part of each of us that puts on the shows: the one that gets irate, angry, victimized; the one who pounds his fists or who runs and hides, whatever you, I, and each of us has created as our own unique constellation of responses (a.k.a. protection mechanisms) to keep our identities well-guarded and intact.*

thought and the mechanisms of habit that block true freedom of consciousness. Krishnamurti made it his life work to point out how we each become habituated to our own set of conditioned responses. But really, how could it be otherwise?

It is a primordial survival instinct to learn what actions result in survival in the face of threat, and to have the capacity to recall and repeat these strategies in order to secure our lives. It is perhaps not inevitable, but certainly predictable that we extend these habituated strategies from the physical ones: "*don't step in the hot fire*", to the psychological ones: "*don't argue back when Dad's in one of his moods*" (or whatever your version). In both cases, you've learned: "*...or you'll get burned*" (a.k.a., punched out, grounded, etc.).

As we respond more and more automatically out of these conditioned patterns that have served us well in the past, we lose the freedom to respond to life's circumstances with fresh ears, eyes, and choices. Our beliefs and actions become quick and automatic responses based on past experiences. We become reactors, behaving in predictable and characteristic ways. All of us do this, in fact most of the time, without even realizing it. And we become identified with (defined by) these characteristic ways: "*Oh that's Ronda for you!*" (Heard it all my life, as you probably have too, substituting your own name of course.)

Our habituated responses become so automatically ingrained and unconscious that we come to believe that we are simply responding (in those ways that were most successful or least painful in the past) to what life today is sending our way. Many of us in fact spend our entire lives wholeheartedly believing we are simply responding to what life dishes out, rather than recognizing that *how we perceive* the world around us, as well as *how we respond* to it, is a choice, a choice that we have given away to habits based on survival patterns we formed early in life.

The ego isn't of itself bad. In fact, as we noted together previously, our ego does an outstanding job of helping us each establish our identities. But over time we confuse the ego-self with our deeper true Self at its Source. We lose perspective. We become identified with our ego-self; we think that *we are* our habituated identities. This gives the ego—or our self-defining personality habits—a great deal of power and influence. More than power and influence, it becomes our overriding sense of reality.

And this is all fine and good by the ego. As long as we continue to believe that our various protective masks (the characteristic ways we each have developed over the years for presenting "who we are" in the world), are really the truth of who we are, we can maintain a certain feeling of self-protection and stability of self. We can relax into a sense of confidence about who we are vis-à-vis these identities. It is a great relief. It is the inherent desire for homeostasis, for solid, for something real to put our minds around.

And to give it its due, the ego (that which helps us establish and maintain a sense of separate identity) has most often, and for most of us, done a really masterful job making sure we feel well-protected by our sense of solid identity.

But an interesting thing has happened in the process: Just as implied in the biblical statement, *"you were created in the image and likeness of God"*, up steps our ego-self-identity to become a miniature god, as we go about creating our own universe by way of our conditioned perceptions, beliefs, and habitual patterns of response. And so we each come to live within a self-constructed universe of our own patterning. We're really very good at it!

Our self-identity (who we come to believe that we are) gives us a needed sense of stasis in a moving, constantly changing world. It helps us "keep it together", but at a price. The price? We forget the freely moving consciousness that originally existed before these self-created personality habits became ingrained.

For the sake of gaining a sense of stability in the world, we sacrifice a larger freedom of being—one that exists as a *quality of presence* within an ever dynamic and living universe. And we replace this more organic, original quality of being that lives in a fluid and changing world, with our preference for a pre-defined identity and a set of more static belief systems about the world and its order.

Quite literally, the ego in its long, arduous, and lustrous career helping us to become self-aware individual beings, establishes itself at the seat of power. And as a *mini-God play ("in the image of")* the ego as sovereign is endlessly clever in its ceaseless attempts to keep as its own, the throne that rightfully belongs to our Soul; our Original Nature. In short, we've become identified with our personalities, and we've forgotten *who we really are*.

We hide really well: We create a box in order to make sense of life and our place in it, put ourselves into that box...and then forget that we have done so. The box becomes our truth. And then we eventually and slowly begin the process of opening the box, and Remembering...

◆   ◆   ◆

THE RIGHT TO CHOOSE (A CONTEMPLATIVE INTERLUDE):

So here we are, in life. Amazing things all around us. The makings of heaven and earth; the makings of God and man: Porsches, cell phones, laptops, preying mantis, hummingbirds, our pet cats and dogs. Olympic athletes, MTV, virtual reality shows, classical guitarists, pedophiles playing priests, mothers nursing new life. Mountains and forests still not penetrated by man, rain forests not yet destroyed, sea life not yet discovered, universes within universes—unimaginable! And these, just the objects…What of the infinite array of circumstance?

Right this second, a cacophony of life's happenings: several hundred new births, and as many conceptions; a few hundred murders and rapes; people laughing, people crying out in despair. People waiting in line at the airport (taking off their shoes), millions in cars and transit; those dining with a lover, chanting in temples, planning a gang bang, selling dope to kids; those camping with their families, pulling weeds from their gardens, bathing their dogs; those glued to the TV, reading the news, donating their time to a cause; those dying of cancer; those in the hair salon, at the grocery store, sitting in their office chairs; those worried about their children's safety; those afraid to know the truth and turning the other way; those gunned down by warring religions; those saving a child from a burning house; those burned out and hung over; those making love on a leisurely Sunday morning.

Here we are, in a teaming pool of All: "the good, the bad, and the ugly" (*tick tick tick*—each split second one more birth, one more death). And here are you and here am I, each aware of our own reality, each attendant to our own circumstance, as if the rest of it were some intellectual exercise. We know it is happening, but it is impossible for us to fully grasp. All we seem able to truly grasp is our own experience, our own universe in which I am the center of mine, you of yours. In this regard, truly we are each a universe unto our self. Each of us filling the screen of our attention with those things we desire, worry over, feel a responsibility toward—filled with those things that are "happening *to* us". Each of us filling our days and moments with the "things" of our own world.

I was speaking with friends last night as we sat by our fire sipping wine. That was the entire universe, our full sense of the reality of the moment, even though countless other circumstances were playing out all around us, in each neighbor's home, throughout the world of experience, and in countless universes beyond.

We were speaking about choice in matters of pregnancy. One friend relayed the story of a bad amnio report she was given during the first trimester revealing a chromosome disorder that indicated some unidentifiable birth defect, and her conscious decision to open to life and whatever was brought into her reality as a result. The other friend said that she realized she could not handle again her extreme bio-chemical post-partum depression, and certainly would not carry to term a child destined to some possible birth defect. It was a charged debate. People usually fall pretty strongly on one side or the other.

However, my point in bringing it up is not to discuss the (often heated) issue of abortion and choice. My purpose here is to use this conversation as a metaphor for looking into how and where we each make our decisions to "abort" or allow life as it presents itself.

On the one hand, it seems we are ultimately called to open to life, to re-establish the capacity to allow life in with all its richness and uncontrolled freedom of expression; to move beyond our limited need to protect, defend, and fight against the reality of an ever-changing world. This (at any rate) is certainly the deepest meaning of spiritual wisdom and the journey toward re-awakening into God-consciousness.

On the other hand, we can only be where we are. We can't force our evolution. We can only become conscious and truthful within ourselves as to where we are in our capacity and desire for true relationship to life, and let that light of awareness lead us toward the undefended self who lives freely in Love.

Can you say that one of us is better, and the other less so, simply because of where she is on the journey? Ultimately not. Ultimately, each can only be where he is. Ultimately each of us is called to face the truth in ourselves: the ways we still hold back from life out of self-protective defenses and fear, and the ways we are able to open to a genuine and always new (undefended) relationship to *what is*, within each moment of living.

It is quite an awesome calling to surrender the defenses of our self-identified universe in favor of a larger, freer relationship to all of life. We're asked to take down the walls surrounding the castle we built, thinking to protect our hearts. The notion of dismantling these walls evokes a great fear of attack and annihilation, and at the same time, a deep longing for the fullness of life that exists beyond the walls restricting us to the castle grounds.

Here you are, and here am I, each within the universe of our own reality, somewhere along the path of remembering who we really are. And each moment of living we are literally presented with *choice*: choice to take down one, three, an entire wall of fears and belief structures that make up the wall surrounding our castles, or choice to reinforce the walls, shore them up, make them bigger and stronger, able to withstand that which is outside and unknown. Each moment, and in a multitude of daily circumstances, life presents to you, *choice:* choice to abort (by way of superimposed belief systems and pre-determined characteristic responses) that which is presently offered by life, or choice to surrender into and meet freely and newly (without prior belief or conditioned patterns of response) that which presents itself.

Here we are, presented with freedom of choice (free will). Here we are with a strong sense of need to protect our castles of self-constructed reality, and yet with a deep yearning to be free of the walls we have constructed around our hearts, and play instead in the open fields of *All* that is Life.

Sooner or later, one comes to see and acknowledge his choice in this matter. Sooner or later, one comes to realize that there *is* a castle and a wall, and vast mysterious fields of life outside the fortress gates. This realization of position and choice is the Calling to Remember. It is inevitable because we are inherently *more than* the life we have constructed inside the castle walls. We were born outside the walls, but have forgotten.

In the act of seeing and acknowledging choice, one comes to stand in her own truth. And upon standing in one's own truth of choice, is the Call to Remember heard again, at long last.

> *"I am the truth, the light, and the way."*
> 　　　　　　　　...Standing in one's truth, is the light, and the way.

This standing in conscious awareness of one's truth (all of it: "the good, the bad, and the ugly") reveals infinite potential; it sheds a light onto the darkness; it reveals the self-created castle for what it truly serves (fear); it offers the possibility of letting go of a few more bricks in the wall of our self-protective identity structures, in order to live and breathe in greater life and freedom.

On the course of evolution toward remembering who we really are, there is an infinite steady stream of human condition at various places all along the trail. Each can only be where he is. This is why humanity can only be "saved" one soul at a time. To the extent one can know and reflect the honesty of his awareness, he becomes a beacon calling another toward her fundamental truth on the journey of ever awakening. Trying to "fix" the conditions of humanity in any other way, while perhaps a band-aid or soothing gel, does not induce fundamental transformation of consciousness. This is a soul-by-soul reclamation. The only change agent is the integrity with which each of us reflects (by our conscious actions and deeds) the truth of where we stand on our journey. *"And the truth shall set you free."*

How shall you live? Are you ready to recognize the castle you have constructed in order to protect (and block) you from the fullness of life that exists outside of those walls, or do you prefer to stay behind the (seeming) safety of these self-created structures of reality? Do you wish to know that which freely lives and grows in fields and vast open spaces, or do you prefer to stay within that which closes out, protects and holds away, letting in only that which the ego-king deems safe and controlled? The choice is yours (and mine) each moment of each day. And you and I are called, sooner or later, to make that choice, consciously.

These are very serious questions. Your answer to these questions is your *living prayer*. By your answer are you creating (right now) your destiny…

Birthing Narcissus

I look into the cool deep pools
And find
The I that is All:

Mother to the Great Spinning
Long before time thought to tick;

Author of the Eternal Spiral,
Swirling upon and around itself
In Endless free-fall
Of Form meeting Form:

> Dancing,
> Struggling,
> Crying,
> Worshiping,
> Hoping…

All *This* that *Is*,
Servicing Her languid delights.

She gazes, incessant
Into these portals of hope;

Delighting in Herself,
Time and Time eternal,
In these liquid spinning orbs
> We call I and Other.

4

The Calling

How does one move beyond the walls of self-protection and open to the vast and mysterious fields of Living Presence?

Clearly the most fundamental and most difficult process is this: realizing that you do indeed have unconscious automatic patterns and subconscious responses to life that keep you within the confines of walled and repetitive realities. (Clue: what are the hurts of your heart?)

You don't have to sit in therapy for years trying to identify and pick apart all your subconscious patterns. You just have to know that you have them, and that they define the structure of your castle walls.

I believe that this initial stirring of movement that brings us to realize the castle walls of our ego-identity, springs from an innate desiring for, and sensing of, our more natural freedom. It is the inherent tug of the heart to express and to know itself within a vastly free expression—one that is in dynamic relationship to a vibrant and constantly new, living moment. It is Life as Source of All, desiring to see Itself and not some stagnate replica of life that is managed from behind the façade of our prefabricated castle walls.

One moves beyond the confines of the self-created fortress, by desiring to explore and know the freedom and mysteries of life that exist outside the castle walls; by desiring freedom more than the "safety comforts" of that which is known within the fortress; in fact, by realizing that your heart (while perhaps protected) is no longer free.

It is a movement of the heart (not the mind) that initiates all transformations awakening to its Source. It is the corrected placement of our deepest sense of yearning and the longings that we so often try and feed by beefing up the coffers.

Let me offer this simple tale by way of parable:

> Once upon a time was a new being brought to life. She was free of spirit, sleeping in tall grasses along a riverbank, and listening to the music of the wild.
>
> Soldiers of the king's army, while keeping lookout for enemy one day, stumbled upon the little babe, and fearing she might be devoured by wild wolves, they brought her into the castle to be cared for and protected by the civilized royal family.
>
> Growing up, the girl soon forgot the memories of early life in the wild, though she'd often have strange dreams of places and things never seen inside the high castle walls. When she mentioned these, she was always warned to "*hush*", and soon she became absorbed in her schooling and life's bustling activities within the castle grounds.

And me, oh my, castle life is quite entertaining! We keep ourselves well supplied with indulgences, diversions and dalliances of all sorts within these confined walls of self-constructed reality. Just look at all of the stories we create and then blow up into big *gala events* within the hallowed halls of "our castles" (complete with guest lists, balloons, full orchestra, and oh, "*whatever shall I wear?*"). Look at how we fret over this concern, gossip over that tidbit, put on performances of all sorts to stave off the boredom and full realization of being so confined. If we can just keep up the appearances....

> [Here's an intriguing experiment: Take a month off from watching any TV and then turn it on again. Our preoccupations (what we make our gods) will be startlingly clear.]

But there are days (and they seem to become more frequent) when we tire of these diversions; we get bored by all the feigned ceremony for the same old dinners in the same old rooms. We yearn to know what lies outside these walls. There is a curiosity that grows, almost like a pale memory. We start to pay more attention to what the ego-king allows to come in through the gates, and we're enthralled to know more. We hear the tales of storytellers and mystics who speak into the dark of night, and our appetite for castle life becomes stale. We long to taste something real again. We long for adventure and the unknown mysteries. We long to shed our prim and proper dress, and slip out some night with one of the bards....

"But, how shall I live outside of these walls? How shall I find shelter and the comfort of these over-stuffed chairs? What if there are dark creatures and dangers I know nothing of? The protection of these walls is all that I know. I fear I should die if I ventured outside.

Yet, look at these magnificent tapestries and paintings; they loom so vibrant and glorious on these cold and gray walls! They tell stories of wild things living free.

And I've heard the songs of the poets. They break my heart, as if I too have known something of their exquisite elixir before these walls, something forbidden and free. Oh, I long to walk barefoot along the vast open fields. I long to lie in the tall grasses beside a cool running stream. I long to take it all in: the smells and the tastes of that which is living free. If only I could remember my way...."

And one day, by such longing, so we all shall.

◆　　　◆　　　◆

Much as we don't want to see it, we're dealing with something—something deep and primordial—something that can never be satisfied within the ego kingdom. That which we seek is not inside the gate.

This dawning of realization that there is something that cannot be known from within the safe boundaries of the ego structure is infuriating, intolerable, and largely denied by the ego-king, ever determined to maintaining the protective walls of reality and purpose. In fact as this realization—this calling of the heart—becomes more clear, our self-created identity structures exhibit all sorts of signs of pressure: cracks in the plaster, leaky plumbing, loose fixtures...and an array of cover-ups to minimize these appearances: paintings hung over cracks, new paint jobs, dim candlelit dinner parties, etc. Quite ingenious, really.

In a thoughtful and luminous book, *The Second Miracle*, author and teacher Richard Moss, M.D., refers to this deep yearning to remember—and the often just as deep or deeper despair that comes as one realizes that this yearning is something that is beyond the walls of our self-created identity structures—"the wound we cannot heal." It is a wound in the sense that it is something that finally breaks through the façade of the ego. It is something in us that is "more than" the ego. It is a part of us that is fundamentally *prior to* the formation of ego. The ego is mortally wounded by this realization that there is something "prior to" its existence. It blows the whole façade.

"Wait a minute! Prior to me?...If there is something prior to me, something prior to my entire structured identity and reality, well then, that can only mean...Oh no!" And BAM!

Down come the walls!

And so begins (if we listen) the music of Creation calling us to the homeward journey of remembering who we really are.

The great mystical writings of the world are filled with stories, parables, and myths describing this homeward journey to reclaim one's authentic Selfhood. It is a timeless story and there are many references, in many languages and religions, describing the struggle, the beauty, and the perils inherent to it.

Why should a journey that offers reclamation of one's True Self be perilous? Because, very essentially, we have become servants to that which once served us. And freedom from slavery is never a freedom easily won. (All the more so when self-designed.)

At some point—either after experiencing enough pain where these old ways of responding are no longer working as they once did, by grace, or both—an inkling of some other way of being, a yearning to be more wholly present to Life, steps forward.

And when this happens, the ego (which has served and protected us long and well with the calcification of our identity) must soften in order to allow our larger authentic Selfhood—or Soulful Presence—to emerge. It is a dethroning, of sorts, that occurs.

This dethroning of that which is seated as our very identity, is experienced very much as a "death" for that which must step down. In fact, the tenacity with which this ego-self-identity strives to hold on and survive its position is spectacular and brutal. Truly we are each called to an inner battle of great mythic proportion. In fact our outer enactments and wars are good, symbolic metaphors reflecting the real battles of transformation of humanity, which begin on the inner terrain of each individual heart.

In the inevitable journey to reclaiming our True Self, we begin the great inner transformation. We experience within our own being, the battle of life over death—a surrendering of unconscious habit to conscious presence. (A crucifixion and a resurrection, quite so!)

For each of us, this journey is invariably met with the struggle and suffering that accompanies the fear of annihilation. It can be no other way. Life must penetrate and pierce the shell of our carefully constructed façades in order to be released (reborn) into Freedom.

The journey back to remembering our Authenticity—our remembrance of "*I Am that which I seek*" in what I've come to call "The Great and Godly Game of Hide and Seek"—becomes an inner enacted rebirthing: "*Unless a man dies [to his old self] and is born anew, he shall not enter the Kingdom of Heaven*" speaks directly to this inward journey. Unless and until we lay down our self-constructed reality, we will not know the Truth of our Original Nature.

This is what enlightenment refers to. It is a fundamental change in conscious presence within the (eternal) moment of now. It is the handing over of our self-constructed power to the larger Truth of *who we really are*, always have been, and always will be:

"I AM THAT I AM."

SUGGESTED EXERCISE:
AN EXCURSION FROM THE CASTLE

1. Consider a current life situation or issue as being a castle.

2. Describe what it looks like. How big is your life issue (your castle)? Is it spacious or cramped? Is it noisy or quiet? Is it confused or orderly? Where and when do you feel contented? Where and when do you feel bored? What do you long for? What do you miss? Who or what do you wish to call into your castle? What are some things you want to keep out? (Be as specific as you can.)

3. Now imagine that you are considering giving up this current life situation or issue. Imagine that you are considering venturing out into the unprotected landscape beyond the castle walls. What are you afraid of meeting? What are you afraid you cannot handle? What do you fear could happen to you if you venture outside the castle walls of your current life situation or issue? What do you long to feel? What do you hope to experience? What feeling do you wish to remember?

4. Envision these images and feelings as if you have actually ventured outside the walls of your castle. See yourself encountering that which you fear. See yourself experiencing that which you long for. How does it feel to be free (outside of) your current life situation or issue? Stay out in the fields of your mind's imagining and experiencing these qualities (the fearful and the hurtful) for three or four minutes if you can do so.

5. After you feel you have experienced the landscape outside as fully as you are currently able, consciously decide to return to the castle of your life situation or issue. How do you feel as you start to approach and come closer to the castle walls? How do you feel as you enter and close the gates behind you? What does it feel like to close those gates and to sit inside the fortress of your life situation or issue again? What do you notice about this castle now that you've ventured outside? Is it bigger or smaller than before you went outside? Is it peaceful or stagnant? Vibrant or overwhelming? How do you feel locked once again inside these walls? Do you wish to stay inside? Do you wish to open the gates? Will you venture out again?

If you were free to choose where to be right now, where would you choose? Inside the castle? On the compound grounds? Up on the balcony looking out? Out roaming the countryside? See where you feel you most long to be. This (whatever your response) is the truth of your living prayer as it is right now.

This is how you create your destiny.

5

At the Pillars of Descent

"There comes a time we all know
There's a place that we must go,
Into the soul into the heart
Into the dark."

—Melissa Etheridge, Into the Dark

Perhaps we recognize, deep down, the very miracle of it all. Perhaps there's such a deep humility (somewhere in there) for the grace that ever-patiently waits upon us as we play out our stubborn and magnificent dramas of fear and ego, keeping us carefully gated behind castle walls and still trying to recover from *The Fall* in a flashy showiness of self-sufficiency and feigned disinterest in the freedom outside the gates of our reality.

High maintenance we are. High drama. We're great at it!

And Grace is kind enough to be the perfect audience, offering a well-placed smile, appropriate tear, and playful applause. We're continually seen and served by grace, no matter how flagrantly we deny and ignore—no matter how long we try to prove *"we'll do it fine by ourselves, thank you very much!"*

◆　　　◆　　　◆

HEEDING THE CALL:

It seems that the Soul—the deepest essence of our True Nature—eventually calls out to each of us to *stop, look, listen*…. Or, more probably, our deeper Self is calling all the time, and something finally stirs in our thick skulls to register the call: *"Hello?"*

At any rate, we are invariably called by Life—and in a fascinating array of ways (many none too pleasant)—to seek a deeper truth of Being. We are called to give up the belief that we are merely our ego-identities. And with the giving up of the belief, we also must give up our desire for all of the *kudos* given these ego-identities by our culture. Not fun.

Sooner or later, and in any number of ways, each of us is called to make this journey Home—to step out of the self-defined identities in which we have lost ourselves, and remember *who* we really are. The call to the Journey of Remembering is a calling Home. It is a deep yearning prayer that reverberates through the darkness until it lands upon our path, like a mysterious gypsy holding out a dark and surprising gift of grace. Amazing Grace!

◆   ◆   ◆

Who knows just where, why, or how one actually begins the journey of remembering? Perhaps the journey was begun millions of years ago with the first stirring of life—with the first primordial heartbeat marking the steady cadence of our eventual Homecoming...

I do know that we're, each of us, called to this journey by the voice of our own Sacred Heart, and so we're, each of us, called in unique ways: some by tragedy, a health crisis, or a difficult marriage; some through a special teacher; some who struggle with substance abuse and addiction; some through prayer. But regardless of differences in outer appearance, all (I sense), are led by grace and the stirring of the heart.

MEETING THE DARK NIGHT OF THE SOUL:

There is a refrain in one of Melissa Etheridge's song, *Into The Dark*, that says: *"there comes a time we all know, there's a place that we must go, into the soul into the heart into the dark..."* At some point along the spiritual path of life, each of us is called to face what St. John of the Cross called, "the dark night of the soul". In many of the mystical systems and writings, this is expressed as the great Soul Quest. It is the journey one enters to meet and to slay the many-headed dragon of deception and illusion that harbor one's soul, one's True Self. It is what Joseph Campbell called the "hero's journey" and it is referred to in much of Jung's work with the great mythic stories used as metaphor for our own inner journey of awakening.

When we say someone is experiencing the "dark night of the soul", we are say-ing that she is experiencing a fundamental and existential *undoing*. We're not talking about a mere "blue period" of struggle and turmoil here. All of us from time to time experience dark times where we may feel lost or depressed or out of sync with life for various reasons. But what we're speaking about here is really much more than some dark period where one finds himself in a state of depressed emptiness and confusion, though that is certainly part of it.

What do I mean by *undoing*? I mean meeting up against the place where our standard operating procedures are turned upside-down…useless; where our roles and persona are exposed as eyeless masks; where even our most fundamental beliefs are called into question; where we cry out from the very depths of our being, at the seeming hopelessness of the human condition to rest in an abiding peace.

The dark night of the soul is a fundamental undoing of the very foundation on which we have staked our security. What we once thought of as our secure threshold, has suddenly appeared as a house of cards on a foundation of sand (and the wind has come up). It is an annihilation of ego-identity constructs that precedes an elemental reconciliation with Soul. Or, more pointedly, it is the sur-render of illusion that ushers the re-membering of *who we really are.*

We're talking about a reformation of one's seat of power, an existential surren-der, and a fundamental awakening to Living Presence. It is a surrendering of the concerns of self-identity (*How shall I act to survive and to prosper?*) in preference to the matters of Soul (*What does Life seek to express through me here, now?*).

If we're fortunate (or well-guided in this process), the struggle and the suffer-ing that comes by way of giving up identification with one's ego, is transmuted through prayerful surrender into a radical renewal that arises in conscious awak-ening. It requires willingly submitting to the suffering, crucifixion, and "death" of the ego-self so that the True Self can be re-membered and re-established (res-urrected) in the Fullness of Being—not in a final act, but in a realization that enlivens a continual moment by moment renewal of Living Presence.[1]

I spoke in my introduction of the dangers I feel are embedded in the tendency to make this reformation of the seat of power into an object: "Enlightened". This is a little dicey to properly express. On the one hand there is a radical shift of

---

1. *I do not reference Christianity (used as metaphor herein) to disclaim its authenticity as an actual historic event. Rather, to say that I believe both levels of meaning can coexist within an endlessly layered richness of Creation Consciousness. I believe awareness of God, as highlighted in all of the great religions of the world, will continue to ever deepen as we continue to evolve in our conscious re-membering.*

awareness (I call it "remembering") that must occur, and to occur, the ego-iden-tity structures must surrender. In that way of speaking, there is something that occurs within one's being that is a dawning of realization, an emerging remem-brance of who you really are. The danger comes when we once again try to make the realized experience into a stronghold for re-identification; something to hold on to and re-identify with. Perhaps a good analogy is in the field of quantum physics: We get stuck on seeing the particle and forget that it is also a wave. Always the paradox is the deeper truth.

More accurate is this: While there may be a profound moment of remember-ing (sort of a felt sense of "aha!") in which the ego surrenders to a living realiza-tion of Unity Consciousness, what one naturally reorganizes around (as a result of this experience) is not *living in* a state "enlightened", but rather in a continual process of surrendering and remembering here, now…and now, and again now. It is a fundamental remembering, and then a continual process of remembering to remember.

THE UNIVERSAL JOURNEY TO FUNDAMENTAL REMEMBERING:

Each of us is called (sooner or later) to a fundamental *Remembering of who we really are.* It is a journey that is universal to nearly every religion throughout his-tory—the search to return to and to know ourselves within God-consciousness.

While the voice that calls to each of us is unique and the path to which we are called may look quite different, the things we must face and release are the same for each of us. We are called to make the individual journey that is universal to all. This is why sacred and mythic stories have so much power. They speak to the universal processes at work in each of us. These sacred and mythic stories hold an important key to our wholeness. Whether in the stories of the Bible, the Torah, Bagavad Gita, the Greek myths, Indian folklore, etc., all these great works are guides to the sacred Journey of Re-membering.

There are certain commonalities in all of these stories. Most notably, the myths of virtually every culture and country speak symbolically to the fact that those of us who embark upon the Soul's Journey, are called to stand and face our shadows—i.e., those things within ourselves that we deny, hide from, consider ugly, frightening, or "bad".

We all prefer to deny, cover over, and repress these parts of ourselves that we are afraid of or do not like. But to do so is folly, and over time extracts a heavy cost. Not only do the parts of ourselves we refuse to look at continue to seek and find unconscious ways of acting out, but we can never be fully embraced in the bright light of Self-Realization until we become our Wholeness.

…How can we re-member (reintegrate) who we really are—how can we live in the Fullness of Being—if we ignore, hide from, or deny parts of anything?

The kind of wholeness of which I speak is established by walking in the truth of ourselves, in bearing to see what we don't want to see, in claiming with humility the full range of ourselves: our fears, our feebleness, our prideful ego, and our radiant beauty. "Healing" the unloved parts of ourselves only comes when they are brought into the light of truthfulness. This is not a one-time task. It is a daily moment-to-moment challenge of attention. To live in that daily attention, an awakening to wholeness is necessary. And for wholeness, a descent is required…

AT THE PILLARS OF DESCENT:

The path of Remembering ultimately requires a *descent* into the realms of *unknowing.* It is a process of being so thoroughly undone by a continual onslaught of unpredictable twists and turns in understanding, as to put one on the very razor's edge of sanity. And even there, you can't tell if you've finally fallen over the edge from one moment to the next. And actually, this is *exactly* the place you have to come to with-stand: The precipice of unknowing is where Truth is found. Again and again, the paradox!

"Treacherous" as a word does not do the journey justice. It has to be so. In no other way will the many-headed dragon give up its protective masks so that we can stand in the light of True Self. In no other way will the ego-self-identity surrender its position or purpose…. It is like giving an actor the role of king, only he forgets it's a role; believes he indeed is king and therefore (of course) refuses to be persuaded, cajoled, begged, or bribed off his kingly seat. (He's king for heaven sakes—*"off with your head"* for trying!) It's like that, the journey to Remembering. It takes an overthrow with real finesse to dethrone someone who believes he's king!

From time to time as I wrestled with myself over matters of ego and control, surrender and soul, I found myself spontaneously singing these two lines of a Don Henley song:

"I will not lie down. I will not go quietly."

(…Ain't it the truth!)

PART II

Journey of Remembering...

✦

A Personal Account of the Universal Story

This is a difficult section of this book, difficult because the path to Self-Remembering is such a universal part of the spiritual journey and yet so very personal and utterly devastating. I find no suitable way to hold up a light in this dark terrain than to offer up some of the tormented pieces and parts of myself as I was devoured and crushed. I hope that by sharing some of the confusion, rawness, and blindness that occurred for me along the way, I might offer those in the depths of their own journey into the dark night of the soul some modicum of comfort: a small night light along the slippery footpath.

My story is not offered as a template for you to follow. There are no templates to follow in a journey such as this. Only is there the example of casting the seed of intent (of offering a living prayer) and of the surrendering (over and over again) into the unexpected, uncontrollable movements of Soul as the prayer is made manifest within the Fullness of Being.

6

In the Beginning Was the Word

Something happened to me a little over a year ago, something terrible and marvelous. And I realize now (on the cusp of re-emergence), that I willingly walked into my own "undoing". In fact I prayed for it. But let me back track a bit...

THE MIRACLE OF A TEACHER:

You know that feeling when you read a book that is so closely aligned with your Soul that you feel you are remembering more than reading? That is how I felt when I first read *The Black Butterfly,* by Richard Moss, M.D. There was clarity of insight that resonated with me as Richard spoke of his own experience of radical awakening, something I knew in my bones and my breathing. I was so moved by his writing at that time (even as one who was proudly self-sufficient and anti-teacher), that I sent a little ceramic prayer vessel I'd made along with a simple note of thanks for the book. Little did I suspect I would eventually (and some 10 years later) allow this man into my heart as a teacher and friend.

As I said in my introduction, when it came to teachers, gurus, and group processes, I had a "tude" as they say. I was *all* against it. These things were antithetical to my belief that "All there is to know is within." I still believe this. But I've found there is a role and a reason for a teacher. It has to do with surrender (not of one's self to the teacher) but of *one's self* to *the One Self.* It has to do with setting in soil the seed of your Soul's Calling. It is a form of prayer; a form of worship really. But again, it is not worship of the guru (as is often mistaken). It is worship and communion in the dynamic revelation of the relationship between self and God (or the Lover and the Beloved, to put it another way).

If one's sense of soul is fairly well-grounded already, a relationship to a mentor/teacher can accelerate the prayerful intent of soul. If one does *not* have that grounding and/or if the teacher is not yet fairly well-stabilized in his soul, well then, all sorts of havoc can (and most usually does) arise. Both beings can become lost in diversions of power and ego and false gods for a long long time.

Not consciously knowing so, I tested the waters with Richard several times over a period of 10 years or so. I'd go to a talk or a one-day retreat he was giving. Something always held what, for me, was a very uncomfortable allure to step in deeper. And something else always told me to stand back and wait.

I waited.

Several more years passed with still no interest on my part for groups or teachers *(au contraire,* in fact!) when I received an announcement for a fundraiser in support of Richard Moss Seminars. The weekend event was fairly inexpensive compared to his seminars so I decided it would be a good way to hear him speak (which is always a delight beyond measure, as he is one of the most prolific and brilliant contemporary speakers on matters of psycho-spiritual understanding).

When I went to the fundraiser, I noticed some kind of shift (whether in him, in me, or both). Something didn't tell me to hold back anymore. In fact something told me it was time I take the plunge and see what it was like to experience a (previously dreaded) group process; to see what it was like to sit and let someone *be a teacher* for one (me) "who didn't need anything from anybody" and who preferred to "do it alone".... Yep, the folly of our created self-identities: They'll dog you!

So at the age of 42, I signed up for a 10-day intensive retreat called *Radical Aliveness* that Richard offered in Sedona, Arizona. I came to call it "spiritual boot camp". But that's another story. Let me just say this: *Holy Smokes!* can the man lead a group, and each individual in it, into his own sanctified relationship with Soul. I simply delved into the depths of myself—and there, Richard continually met me with tenderness and a soulful presence grounded in his own humanness.

Let me also just say this (in my moment of impishness provocation): some of the exercises he used to support conscious attention test every fiber of willingness to stay present. Hence my renaming this seminar "spiritual boot camp"...But I'll leave further discovery up to you.

Suffice it to say, after a lifetime of self-sufficiency and running circles around anyone who tried to show me anything (a thinly disguised mask of self-protection, I've only recently come to admit), I met my match. At long last I accepted someone who could meet me with great care, reflection, and humanness; someone with profound insight and shining, perceptive brilliance. At long last I'd grown up enough to let in the mentoring role of a teacher; I'd matured enough to experience the stunning wellspring of my own inner wisdom that arose to meet the personal responsibility of such a relationship...Thank God.

While I've occasionally read devotional books (usually written by devotees of eastern spiritual gurus), and have most often felt (well, quite frankly) like gagging, I've had a change of heart. I've come to appreciate that there are times for the spiritual support of a teacher or guide. And there is a relationship to these times that requires every shred of inner wisdom and maturity that one can bring to bear. I've come to see that there is not a "giving over of me" to a teacher—or even that I need necessarily agree with or approve of some behaviors or imbalances I will surely see in the other, if he allows himself to be honestly seen. There is a deeper current in this mentoring relationship, and it requires a foundation of human honesty and deep personal faith in, and devotion to, the mystery of spiritual intention invoked through relationship.

It is very hard to put accurately into words this kind of relationship. But it is critically important. So many people give themselves away in their misguided attempts to "get it" from a teacher or guru or religion. The induction into a remembering of who you really *are* through relationship to a teacher, a teaching, or a religion, requires a very fundamental honesty and intimacy within yourself. It all starts there. There, and by Grace and the integrity of intention, do miracles of awakening take place.

The best way I can liken the appropriate relationship to a teacher is to compare it with what I consider the proper use of books and religious texts as a teaching or guide. The way I approach a book is to *listen in* to how it stirs my own feeling of remembrance. I note places where it resonates something inside me—could be recognition; could be a question. And where it does stir something, I contemplate it deeply and let it percolate within me until the bud becomes my own flowering of insight and understanding.

This is how I've come to understand relationship to any form of spiritual guidance (be it a religion, a guru, a husband, a child, a book, or an answer to a prayer).

Everything in life, to the receptive heart, has the potential to reveal true spiritual awakening.

To see this; to start to allow the world (and each encounter in it) to be a teaching, is to cast the seed of life onto fertile soil. It sends a prayer of intention for *Truth* out into the vast universe where all prayers reverberate and hasten to reflect. To *seek* in this way is to say: "*I'm here and I'm ready to listen.*" And to listen in this way requires the utmost personal awareness and responsibility for bringing forward one's own inner wisdom in relationship to life. It quickens the soul because it is a living prayer. And true living prayer is always heard.

◆   ◆   ◆

MY PRAYER INTO THE MYSTIC:

Having established my own grounding in spirituality—first through my family upbringing that was very much centered around church and worshipful living, and later through my widening inquiry into many of the world religions, mystical writings, philosophical thought, and the contemporary bridging of psychology and physics—my husband and I entered together into a three-year mentoring program with Richard Moss along with 21 other people, from around the world, who he interviewed and accepted into this process.

On the last day of our first session together, Richard suggested to me that I create a "devotional practice" since I was already naturally doing many of the other practices he was trying to get fellow participants to bring into their lives as part of spiritual growth and well-being: things like spiritual and psychological readings, meditation, physical movement, silence. My first thought at his suggestion was: *"Heck my whole life is a devotional practice. What's he talking about?"* And yes, I do live an unusually peaceful, celebratory communion with life. I express it in my art, my poetry, my cooking. *"Blah blah blah"* says little miss perfectionist. *"I don't need anyone to show me anything (so there)."*

...I decided to listen to him (anyway).

And so when I returned home from the weeklong retreat, I wrote a poem that I converted into a song so that I could sing it as a "devotional practice". It is a song-prayer that speaks in three progressive voices.

> The first stanza is an acknowledgment of the initial wounding we all experience as part of our individuation into self-identity, and a prayerful appeal not to stay lost in this ego identity, but to use the wound to return to Source; ("...*cast me not from your caress my frail and feeble ways; but lifted be my woundedness to your igniting spark, my injury a flaming torch alighting from the dark.*")
>
> The second stanza is a prayer of affirmation and recognition of Source as it stirs alive within the body consciousness. It is the resonance that rides on the breath within the experience of meditation, showing us the living metaphor with nature's great timelessness as reflected in

the tide. ("...*Thy breath in me revealing the fragrance of your tenderness, the mystery, your Grace! I come to you with open heart, a movement born of thee; a measure on your timeless path, a wave upon the Sea.*")

And the final stanza is a direct prayer of surrender and intent for the mystic. ("...*ignite me in thy sacred tongue, consume me in the pyre! This cup [me], it is my offering; I lift it to the flame, that I may touch the breath of Truth, and speak thy Holy Name!*")

For the first time in my life I learned the real power of living prayer,

...and the truth of: "Be careful what you ask for!"

I was plunged into a radical Self-Remembering by way of a confrontation with disease and death and then catapulted *("do not stop; do not collect $200")* into the hallowed halls of the *dark night of the soul*, where I met my undoing...

The Offering

Oh blessed Soul
Oh Great Eternal Dreaming
Let this be my prayer:

This vessel, I,
Thy spirit in me resting,
Cast me not from your caress
My frail and fearful ways;

But lifted be my woundedness
To your igniting spark,
My injury a flaming torch
Alighting from the dark.

[Behold, the flame!
Behold the rapture glowing.
Let me steep in thy embrace.
Let me fall into your name.]

Oh blessed Soul
Oh great Eternal Dreaming
Let this be my prayer:

This vessel, I,
Thy breath in me revealing
The fragrance of your Tenderness,
The mystery, your Grace!

I come to you with open heart,
A movement born of thee;
A measure on your timeless path,
A wave upon the Sea.

Oh blessed Soul
Oh Great Eternal Dreaming
Let this be my prayer:

This vessel, I,
Thy fire in me stirring,
Ignite me in thy sacred tongue,
Consume me in the pyre!

This cup, it is my offering;
I lift it to the flame,
That I may touch the breath of Truth
And speak thy Holy Name!

[Behold, the flame!
Behold the rapture glowing.
Let me steep in thy embrace.
Let me fall into your name.]

7

The Veil Is Lifted: Awakening

I was at our family cottage in Skaneateles, New York, surrounded by the comfort of my brothers and sisters, cousins, and ancestors who lived there before me. It is a very special place to me because of the soulful memories I have of sitting on the dock and watching the sunset, or sleeping out under the stars and talking with my sister til near dawn about the concept of infinity, life, God (…and boys).

I had been singing my prayer song regularly for months and was having a running stream of very powerful dreams. So when it came time for my husband and me to return to California, I decided (very odd and unlike me) to stay on for another week and let this process continue.

I still cannot say what happened exactly. One night for no apparent reason and surrounded by family and ancestors, I freaked out; I panicked as something broke loose. The veil was lifted and I came face to face with life in a terrifying and compelling way. Alone in my bed on the sleeping porch, I found myself trembling with an uncontrollable (and "irrational") fear.

As I looked into the face of this fear, I could literally see the exquisite pain and struggling beauty of generation after generation of humanity having tried so long and so desperately, and in so many sad and beautiful ways, to connect in love; to know our inheritance in Source, all the while and simultaneously putting a deep-seated, subconscious fear up as the very barrier to our own deepest longing. It is a tragedy—a "*Divine Comedy!*"

I saw my own (and all of humanity's) absolute desperate desire for love, and the equally deep terror for living that prohibits that which is so desired. In this stunning state of seeing, I was completely overwhelmed by life's unbearable bounty and deep losses. For hours and throughout the night, all I could do was tremble and shake uncontrollably in my bed as my family slept all around me.

Several days later and back home in Ojai working on a conceptual art piece for a fundraiser (a chair titled "Get Centered" and incorporating Chilton Pearce's work: *Crack in the Cosmic Egg*, interestingly enough), I was suddenly struck down with a very bizarre and massive loss of balance. It came on as a sudden exploding in my brain and I was knocked to the ground (literally).

MY DIALOGUE WITH DEATH:

The sudden and violent attack of extreme vertigo (a total loss of equilibrium and balance) is like nothing I'd ever experienced in my life. It came out of nowhere and it came with a vengeance. Then it would just as strangely disappear for a day or a week and I'd return to my normal activities, only to have it return without warning and stay for unpredictable lengths of time.

Often, for days on end, I'd be literally floored and unable to move even an eyeball for the extreme nausea the disequilibria provoked by any slightest movement at all.

This went on for six weeks within the context of a totally sluggish and seemingly inept HMO system that simply wouldn't respond other than sending me hastily to the ER, which would promptly ping-pong me back to the HMO, clearly neither wanting the liability nor the cost of care on their side of this horrendous health care system we pay for.

I existed in a state that was so extreme as to beg evidence of a truly serious and seemingly life-threatening problem, with no diagnosis as to what was happening to me and no treatment (except some sleeping pills which I refused so that I could ascertain what was really happening, or at least so I could remain conscious if "this was it").

I have always had a very high discomfort tolerance, an athletic attitude of "no pain, no gain". But this was something beyond discomfort. It was so severe I felt quite certain that I must be dying of some exploded tumor, and indeed my symptoms pointed to that possibility, as I learned in a desperate attempt to find answers through the download of medical journals and articles on the Internet. At one point I experienced an odd squishing in my neck, and I still hear a constant heartbeat in the left ear…. A good constant reminder of the pulse of life, here, now.

I lived in a state of profound fear and unknowing for over 6 weeks. During part of this time I was completely normal, and then suddenly and without any warning, I'd be hit again. The unpredictability made the grip of terror even worse (like swimming in the ocean and wondering if *Jaws* is down below…*dunt dunt, dunt dunt*).

What was most odd was that if I stayed in one position, not moving my head or my eyes, I'd feel normal. If I moved even the slightest, the sensation of imbalance and nausea would be so severe as to practically render me insane. I learned the fine art of prolonged states of silent stillness while simultaneously being forced to watch the incredible power of fear (in all its showy and subtle forms of finesse) parade through my mind, showing me its teeth and fangs and false smiles. I was the captive understudy to fear. And I was smack-dab in the middle (ear) of a profound awakening experience.

Below are several passages from my journaling during those times I could write. They offer, I believe, something of the rawness of the journey into the primal fear of non-being and, what was for me, the beginning of my descent into the dark night of the soul (although I sure didn't know it then as we rarely, if ever, do).

<u>JOURNAL ENTRY</u> (FIRST EPISODE):

Thursday, and again yesterday (Friday) I was a little dizzy, but it did not escalate. Thursday night I was awakened by an incessant owl. It was eerie to me, given owl mystique, and the health fears coalescing around this past week. I had some kind of odd "visitation"/meditation—not fully awake, but not fully asleep either—whereby I felt as if the owl were a messenger.

The thought came into my mind that this is one of the times that I could die. I then had the thought: *"If I have a choice, and if I pass on this opportunity to die, I have no idea what trauma or difficulty or innumerable suffering, out of my control, may be in store for me by continuing to live."*

I felt as if I were being called to make a conscious decision: to come to realize that "to live" means once again to consciously face the fear of life, living, death, dying; to declare living, means consciously doing so this time, and with all the fear of the unknown that comes with it.

That is a scary realization. It is again facing that (in fact) every moment of living is grace—none of it is a guarantee…I'm so terrified by the unknown and so enraged at my inability to control/protect my future!

I looked at (or perhaps dialogued with) this "awareness", and I determined that I'm not ready to die. With this conscious feeling of: "even with this unbearable terror of the unknown, I still wish to live" came the further provocation:

"Well then, if you aren't ready to die, what is it you live for; to what purpose?…"

JOURNAL ENTRY (ONE WEEK LATER):

At 3:30 A.M., I almost called for Steve to take me to the hospital again. There is nothing on this planet I am more afraid of than going to the hospital. I went to bed about 6 P.M., with pretty strong vertigo. At 3:30 A.M., it was so strong as to waken me from a deep sleep. I was scared, and yet I couldn't fully feel the fear either. Odd.

I got kind of freaked by all the "coincidences": staying extra with Mom and Dad at the cottage (was I saying goodbye?); the owl messenger (many say that the owl comes to usher in a death); my conversation with Julia yesterday about having achieved a place of freedom in life that everyone is striving to reach, and my being afraid to claim this privilege for fear that then some force will come in and (Wham!) snap it away. (…Why did I just yesterday have that particular conversation?) This is nerve racking.

I've tried and tried to sort out a medical explanation of what's going on. I've "tried on" all sorts of things: brain tumor, inner ear infection, hepatitis, etc. etc. I've tried on psychological/biochemical explanations like something changing in my wiring. I've tried spiritual faith—i.e., letting it usher in my prayer for realization (and not hindering or stopping it with fear or grasping at these other explanations).

I've watched all of this. I want an explanation so I know "what I should do"—i.e., if it's hepatitis I'd darned well better get thee some medical care. If it's a ruptured eardrum—same. And yet I also realized I don't have to "do" anything, nor do I have to have an explanation, except from the position of fear of not staying alive and well…and to assuage that part of me that tries to believe I was ever really in control of this anyway.

I started to panic as all this was coalescing about me—panic that I might actually be dying. (Well I am. We all are. Who's to say when or how?!) It's positively terrifying (yet I can't really feel it). The blow of death's inevitability and not knowing the when and how, is really freaking me out.

I tried accepting life as it is here, now. I tried accepting whatever comes that I'm afraid of: death, dying, disease, having to go to the hospital—LIFE OUT OF MY CONTROL!

Part of me could do this. I also hoped for some "grand realization" or "transformation". Everyone says it's not possible through the mind, so how would I know? Maybe I had one…

Can I just let life live me, and fall into what Deepak Chopra calls "spontaneous right action"? When I began to drift back to sleep I realized as I did so: "Well, if I do have some really escalating problem and I fall into a coma or into paralysis, I guess there'll be a spontaneous right action that will follow…"

I went back to sleep conscious of truly not knowing if I was at the ending of my life! That is so weird to contemplate. And its contemplation did not bring about any peace. I could clearly see the fact that I have no real control over my life and how, when, or why it ends—and I could sort of "rest into that", but not with any great "*ah ha*" insight or rushing realization "that we're all One". Nope. No such luck…I fell back asleep in the hands of "just not knowing" if I'd be alive, dead, or somewhere in between in the morning.

During this time of inexplicable illness, and on days when I could bear to sit up and write, I would sometimes experiment with automatic writing as a way to try and gain access to some deeper channel of understanding about what was happening to me.

One thing that has intrigued me for years is the amazing intelligence I learned we can tap into through the use of *automatic writing*. For anyone who has not done it, automatic writing is just that. You simply pose questions to yourself, and let whatever instantly and freely associates, speak. The real trick to automatic writing is to write as quickly and as mindlessly as you can.

I was first introduced to this incredible process in a book by Sondra Ray entitled, *I Deserve Love*. And I recommend trying it! A woman in a workshop with me asked about automatic writing, and I showed her the excerpt below. Stunned, she thought I had some kind of channeled prophet speaking through me until she shyly tried it herself (and realized she has her own prophet as well!)

The section below offers, I think, a good example of the amazing wisdom we each carry within ourselves. I rarely realize what is coming out as I am doing the automatic writing. It is later, when I look back to digest and take in what was written, that I am often astonished and carried to a new level of insight as well. This was certainly the case with my automatic writing during this horrendous dialogue with death.

JOURNAL ENTRY (WEEK THREE...AND THE BEAT GOES ON):

Four days or so since my last entry. Have had strong vertigo non-stop now for over 48 hours. Quite draining. I'm discovering from Internet research that "most often" this is middle ear problem, and "most often" it is called "benign positional vertigo" (as opposed to infection or brain tumor, etc.). However the sluggish HMO money machine has yet to do any of the key tests to help properly diagnose. So I've decided to go with the most likely and have started doing my own tests and positional treatments as found on Internet articles by two vertigo neurologists.

What are some possible metaphoric meanings?

> *"I need to stop (slow down) and pay more attention to my inner ear."*
> *"I need to learn new balance."*
> *"I am imbalanced."*
>> *("Get centered" is the title of the chair sculpture I made*
>> *and donated during this time. Coincidence?)*
> *"Balance your actions by listening to your inner ear."*
> *"Learn a new way of looking at the world."*
> *"It's all tenuous."*
> *"My inner ear is changing my outer perspective."*

...I could say any of these may be true...I'll try automatic writing.

AUTOMATIC WRITING FROM MY JOURNAL:

[Note: In this passage, the questioner in the process (me) is denoted by "Qu" and the immediate automatic response I receive from my inner voice, is denoted by "A".]

Qu: *What is this dizziness about for me?*

> **A:** "It's about your courage, about staying on course.
> It's about finding a new way."

Qu: *What kind of new way—or how can you speak more about it?*

A: "New balance points—more steady even in the midst of disarray. Able to move when you're not in control. It is an inner flexibility. It is a teacher."

Qu: *Can I do something more or different to hear and integrate the teaching better?*

A: "Don't get too distracted with other things. Let your consciousness rest in the discomfort without getting totally restricted around it.
Let it be. Move with it. Rest with it. Open to it."

Qu: *How can I better open to this?*

A: "Just like you're doing so far. Be open with it, open with others talking about it. Writing. Dreams, of course. See that what you're doing is right: you're not overly pushing your will to understand or explain, but you're not diverting your attention away from it either. You simply and simultaneously live in/with it—paying attention but not with any driving mission to understand it. This is where Richard was telling you to reside when he spoke of being patient and letting life move through you. This is what you are now learning."

Qu: *I seem to have already learned this on so many levels—like my approach to work and my ways of living?*

A: "Yes, but all those are within the bounds of your self-created comfort zone. You know you have a deep-seated fear of discomfort and things out of your control. What is this ear thing?"

Qu: *Uncomfortable and out of my control! Frightening.*

A: "Right. And still you're learning to adjust (rebalance) to these conditions. You've not felt forlorn, helpless, or overly fearful throughout. You've met the experience, questioned it "lightly" and let it move as it moves. That is the lesson right there.

Again, you didn't try and force some grand enlightenment or resolve, but rather responded by living in openness (even to fear and dying).

That is the course-way of truth. That is the wind of wisdom in
your sails that keeps you on the course-way of truth and living in
the openness and fullness of Being."

Whew! This still astonishes me. By engaging myself in this automatic writing,
I was able to tap into a deep wisdom (call it collective consciousness, God, inner
knowing, or the deep intelligent Current of Life) that is ever available to each of
us. And by tapping into this wisdom, I was able to stand outside of myself and
become transformed. I was able to move to a new level of awareness. I was listening to life and letting its deep current carry me to Source.

And you can do it, too!

◆   ◆   ◆

My hope (and the intent in sharing this story of my own conscious awakening) is that you use my thoughts and examples to facilitate your own engaging
process of self-inquiry and celebration on the never-ending journey of radical
awakening into the *remembering of who you really are*. These are universal principles in the course-way to self-realization:

fear,   Love.
non-being,   awakening,
surrender,

It is a matter of where we each choose to place the fulcrum of our attention:
"*To what purpose do I consecrate my living? What do I make my god?*"

We make gods of all sorts of things: our careers, our passions, our addictions,
our bodies, our possessions, our doctors, our religious leaders, the Internet.

I could easily explain away my vertigo experience this way: *an inner ear infection caused by diving at our lake followed by a cold virus and the air flight home, thus
creating a condition of "benign positional disequilibria"*. I could also focus my
attention on the fact that it cost me a significant loss in client business, or on the
financial loss of family security, the upset relationship it created with my husband, etc. I could wrap myself very easily in the medical labyrinth, taking test
upon test to rule out some deep abiding disease process in an attempt to assure
the security of my life.

Or, I can take this same encounter and attend to what the experience seeks to
awaken in me, without attaching to some belief in order to "*explain it*". I can

attend to being present simply to *what is.* I can look and see if I am able to be fully alive in relationship to that *which is.*

"How present to life do you dare be?"

In this case, I was called to be present and in intimate relationship with the fear of disease and dying.

The previous examples of various levels of attention that one might give this situation (the loss of business, getting to the bottom of a medical diagnosis, etc.), are not false so much as they are removed from the actual intimacy of being present in relationship to that *which is,* here, now.

These are fundamentally different orientations of presence. One seeks to control and protect identity; the other seeks to surrender into what Life is seeking to awaken in the form of dynamic relationship and awareness.

This is in fact, the key right here to awakening. It is within the ordinary life circumstances that come our way as part of our daily living—and how we *choose* to relate to them.

How will I choose to relate to life's situations? Will I listen merely to the superimposed explanations, fears, and belief systems, or will I choose instead, to simply stand in direct relationship with *what is?* The former (buying into the explanations, the stories we tell ourselves, the fears) is how we most commonly relate to life when unaware. This latter (standing in direct relationship to *what is*), is the way we're called to relate to life, in awakening to who we really are. This does *not* mean you don't address valid concerns or explanations. They simply do not take up the full screen of your attention. They are no longer simply an unconscious reaction to the stories we tell ourselves. Rather, one's field of attention is broadened and given into conscious relationship with that *which is,* at its root and prior to the smaller, more constructed explanations we create and superimpose.

In a poetic letter from Richard Moss, sent to those he works with and posted to his web site just after the bombing of the U.S. World Trade Centers (which occurred at the same time I was experiencing the vertigo), he said this of fear:

> "Fear is a great god in our subconscious minds. Fear rules us the moment we lose contact with our own deepest being, the moment our own survival as a creature or an ego becomes more important than the truth of love and the deepest values and principles that can guide our lives."

He went on to say:

> "Fear tricks us with hope. It tells us we can survive, be in control, feel safe if we have the right weapons, enough wealth, enough power, the "right" group of true believers.
>
> ...Spirituality is not an answer to fear, but a choice to be in relationship to fear and not to become a victim or hand servant to fear's agenda.... Spirituality has never been about survival, never been about bowing to fear. It has always been about a relationship to life in the present moment and about the simple fullness of being.
>
> We cannot oppose fear on fear's terms; to do so is to surely lose. Rather we must remember what really matters and live in such a way that we become transmitters of faith in Love's slow but inexorable redemption of fear."

Yes.

As I grappled with the fear of my own dying—as I lived in relationship to it—the fear did not go away; it was not controlled or abated by this willingness to enter relationship. In fact it led me deeper into a full-on realization of my absolute existential terror over the fact that I cannot (nor can any of us) control or ultimately protect ourselves from our own imminent death.

The primordial fear of non-being is so wired within this ego-body-identity we call "I", as to render the very notion of death completely inconceivable. I cannot accept (much less understand) the notion of my "non-being". And yet we know the body is mortal. Mortality is a terrifying construct for the ego-universe we have come to in-*habit*. (As Richard said in his letter "...*to oppose fear on fear's terms, is to surely lose*.") The tricks and turns of the mind to try and do anything but accept the inconceivable and terrifying fact of physical non-being (death of the body) and the truth of the mystery of the unknown, is one of the world wonders to behold. It is ceaseless. It is the basis upon which our religious beliefs and warring dogmas are created over and over again. Fear comes in on top of a religion based on love. We doom ourselves in fear every time we deny or fight against it.

It is futile. It is the wrong approach, these desperate attempts to control or resolve the fear so we can feel "unafraid", safe. Can you see the impossibility of it? You can't ever embrace love if it is motivated as a means to make the fear go away. When the motive for love remains fear-based, *Bzzzt—busted!* (Believe me, I tried it all.)

There is only acknowledging and consciously feeling the fear. There is only giving up the fight against it. There is only fully, vulnerably meeting and being in awareness of it.

When one comes to stand in aware relationship with fear (or anything else), he suddenly has the opportunity to discover himself as *more than it*, by way of having moved his awareness outside of it in a sense.

Question: Where are you do you suppose when you stop resisting, and instead surrender into aware relationship with "*what is*"?

…You are embraced in the Eternity of Love, in a moment, an instant, in the twinkling of an eye. In an instant, you are re-established within Eternal Presence—you are "*That* which is conscious of *this* which is arising, here, now."

Is that a paradox, or what? How can standing in conscious relationship to the fear take you out of its grips? It's like the Chinese finger puzzle: As long as you try to pull your fingers apart (and the harder you try), the tighter the grip. When you stop trying to pull them apart, and move toward (surrender into) the puzzle, you are released into freedom!

…That, is the subtlety of awakening into the Fullness of Being!

SUGGESTED EXERCISE:
A PROPHET SPEAKS (AUTOMATIC WRITING)

Take 10 minutes, find a starting question of deep personal concern or interest (something you're fearful of is always a good bet). Let your brain go blank, and your fingers FLY! (*Just do it!*)

8

Coming Undone

o o o o o o o o o o o o o o o o o o o o o o o o o o o o o o o

"She's come undun,
She didn't know what she was headed for,
And when she found what she was headed for,
It was too late."

—*The Guess Who, Undun*

When one enters the dark night of the soul (however he has come to this precarious precipice), it seems that he has to walk the trail almost completely blinded, only seeing what is met on the path well after it has already been left behind (as if our eyes have been re-moved to the back of our heads). My own experience is surely this.

In hindsight, wisdom comes. But at the time of the falling, *Nada! Zip! Big confused blank.*

◆   ◆   ◆

Little did I know after issuing my living prayer for meeting my Soul's intent, and the events that followed—the strange and terrifying lifting of the veil at our family cottage, the bizarre encounter shortly thereafter with an extreme vertigo and many long hours contemplating and watching the fear it inspired—that I was experiencing answers to my prayer in full action. Little did I realize, at the time, that I had entered into what St. John of the Cross called *the dark night of the soul,* and was in the process of coming "undone". Like the old song from The Guess Who: "*...and when [I] found what [I] was headed for, it was too late.*"

To cut to the chase, with the onset of my bizarre and sudden vertigo, everything in my life came to a screeching halt, and it didn't start back up again when the vertigo had passed. There was no more back to busy-ness as usual. Some part of me was aware of the significance of what I had prayed for—and that "part of me" made a willing surrender into a contemplative relationship with non-doing—with "being a nobody".

But I did it kicking and screaming, too. This is difficult to express, but it is important to shedding light on the subtle dynamic of surrender and control that we all bounce back and forth between. It is the ground where ego-identity and soul go into battle for the seat of our attention. It is the fundamental undoing of ego-identity that ushers in the truth of *who we really are*. It is the hero's journey into battle to slay the many-headed dragon of illusion so that the heart can be released into freedom in our Fullness of Being. It is the true meaning of "holy war". And a holy war it is.

I relay my own experience of this holy war between ego and soul (control and surrender, death and life), with the hope that by sharing some of the confusing tapestries I encountered, you may better wrestle through the subtleties of your own.

THE ORIGINAL PRAYER:

I make one keystone here, having come to some vantage point on my path: I am absolutely sure that the only thing that "saves" any of us from the powerful grasp of fear, ego, and the illusion of separateness, is living prayer.

It was not by the prowess of my clever mind, nor the help of friends, family, teachers, yoga, deep breathing, saints or sages that I was led by grace to meet my-Self in Source. It was by the thread of my sincere prayer for the mystic that my faith was strengthened to follow (even without hope) the hands of Grace that were all the while holding me.

It is only now, in hindsight, that I've come to know this truth. The prayer is the seed of your redemption into Wholeness. The prayer is "the Word" cast upon a fertile soil. ("*And the word was made flesh and dwelt among us.*") Without the willing surrender that is implicit in offering up a sincere living prayer, the quest is futile and incomplete (I might even dare say "fraudulent").

What do I mean by a *living prayer*? I mean one that is imbued with your deepest intent; one that is infused by the willing worship of your living. To offer a true living prayer, one must contemplate deeply what matters in life—to what one is in service. And from that contemplation, will arise a true living prayer, what I sometimes call the *original prayer*; that which reverberates into the void of infinite potential (as Deepak Chopra puts it), and calls you to Remembering. It is a sacred pact, a fulfillment of destiny.

Am I saying, *"I've arrived; I was undone and now I'm done—complete?"* No, I surely am not. I don't believe there is any such "arrived" in that sense. There is only a continual opportunity for choice in renewing and surrendering into the Original Prayer. It is a life-long (eternity-long?) process of surrendering into unknowing, so that Truth can be known. Now how's that for something the mind can never really get?

Can you live within a Wisdom that the mind cannot fully grasp?

This is what is asked of you in the process of Remembering.

◆   ◆   ◆

In my own experience, it was the seed of my living prayer—that which came from the very primordial depths of my yearning—that brought me into the cave of undoing and (eventually) into the wisdom and renewal "that surpasses all understanding".

PLAYING CHESS IN SPADES AND HEARTS:

Here's how I can analogically relay the experience of being undone; of meeting the dark night of the soul. For me, it was a sometimes-subtle dance, and at others, an out-and-out mud wrestling game of power and politic between ego and Soul. To continue the metaphor of the ego getting the starring role as king and then forgetting it's only a role and refusing to come down from the seat of power, there was for me, a constant battle as to *who is,* and *who is not* sitting on the throne of my awareness.

Beginning with the issue of my living song-prayer *The Offering*, that which stands "prior to" the identification of ego was invited to take up residence at the throne of my awareness. That is, I asked that my awareness of God-consciousness be that upon which my life is referenced—the highest purpose to which my life stands. And *swish,* in came Soul! Fine and good thus far. Problem is, my ego, very much believing himself the true king, and believing further (the arrogant little *&@$# that he is) that the very "Kingdom of Ronda" depends on his remaining sovereign, had no intention whatsoever of handing over the throne to Soul. To ego, Soul is an unwelcomed, highly undesirable, very threatening and deadly public enemy number One!

Well, perhaps you can imagine the battle that ensued. A great game of chess transpired: pawns were sacrificed and thrown around like mad, bishops cornered, tortured and released to send a message back to the opposing king; knights were taken and locked up; each check on the queen resulted in another flourishing maneuver that would put Bobby Fisher to shame.

Then it got dirty. Squares were painted, queens were disguised as their opponents, bishops dressed in drag. (Ok, so I have a little fun now. It was NOT so then!) It became in fact, impossible to tell which side was which, who was seated on the throne, if the game was over, if both sides had kissed and made up, or if everyone was just breaking for tea. It was like Alice in Wonderland meets Alfred Hitchcock.

I offer some humor by way of analogy here, because I discovered that a big part of traversing this treachery is loosening up on one's perspective. There was a constant call for flexibility on rough and changing ground lest I fall off the cliff taking the board and all its pieces with me (as in "off my rocker, nobody home"). Could have happened.

Now, let me take you a little closer to the terrain…

THE FINE ART OF NON-DOING AND BEING NOBODY:

Having understood the dynamics of how we forget our true self through our identification with ego-identity and its protective habitual patterns of response—and having intuitively recognized as well, the universality and importance of the hero's descent into the dark night of the soul in order to reclaim wholeness—all I can say to you is that *some part of me* held the rest of me pinned to the void of non-doing and would not allow me the relief of identity, or action, or of "being somebody", no matter how loudly I cried "uncle". Let me give a few examples.

At the time I owned my own research consulting business of over 18 years, which had always made an easy, good living without too much effort. It stopped. I was fairly well-known regionally as an artist doing large installation performance projects as well as sculpture in my own studio. Never before had I gone more than a couple of weeks without creating. I stopped. In fact, I stopped everything except getting groceries and running in the mountains with a girlfriend a couple times a week. I literally wandered around my home everyday for hours on end, days on end, weeks and months on end. I would sit sometimes in our chair on the deck for hours doing nothing, thinking nothing, not meditating, just "hanging out" in nowhere land. I would wander aimlessly from upstairs to down, from inside to out. This went on for well over a year.

Stop! Don't even go there!

Don't even say: "*Boy, I wish I-I-I-I could afford that luxury!*"

I know you think you do, but fact is, you don't. Fact is, no one really does. That's why we keep so many diversions and things "we simply have to do" up and in the way of meeting ourselves alone: empty of identity, diversion, and distraction.

There is nothing pleasant about it. It is the most confronting, difficult place I never wanted to go. But what this prolonged period of no-worldly-identity ("*this is Ronda*") served, in terms of my living prayer, is that of allowing me the opportunity to watch the ceaseless attempts of the ego to try and find, manufacture, and supply identity. Any identity!

Having come to the place where my previous identities had been taken "off-line" (those of artist, business woman, friend, athlete, community helper), I watched the amazing absurdity of those that my poor ego came up with in its desperate attempt to keep me identified (solid, in homeostasis). I had so few diversions of identity, that those of my mind-making filled the screen of my days. It was like one REALLY long brutal meditation. I got to see in full color, uninterrupted panorama, the endless antics of the ego to maintain its position as king.

I watched and watched and watched.

Actually, no. It was worse than that. Some part was watching, and another part was caught up in each and every clever trick and seductive question posed by the ever, seemingly helpful ego:

> "*I'm only trying to help you get what you want—the truth*" it says, as it brings on a new array of possibilities for a grand future: Things like: "*I've got it! Here's your soul's magnificent purpose in life: you're a song-writer, you're a poet, you're a...* " (You fill in the blank; I probably went there!)
>
> Later, when that didn't work, the ego would cleverly say things like: "*You do realize that you're being tricked by some inner wound that wants to self-destruct don't you?*"
>
> Or when that didn't work, I'd hear, in my mind's eye, this little tidbit: "*Don't you see that you're spitting in the very face of God by your slothful inactivity?*" Or (...well, you get the point).

It goes on and on and on. Never stops actually. Each voice looms suave (smooth, real convincing), trying to get you hooked, like being a little kid on a playground and getting seduced by a pusher. It is my variation on the theme of the temptation of Christ by Satan.

And, you know what? This isn't just a past tense story. This is exactly what transpires inside each of us on an ongoing daily basis, each time our ego identities are threatened in any tiny way. We just (and for the most part) haven't become quiet enough to catch the game before we're seduced into it.

In a nutshell, herein lies a big piece of our struggled entrapment and loss of remembering who we really are. We're enveloped in non-stop, seductive, mental white noise that is constantly talking over the deep abiding stillness of our true Fullness of Being.

◆   ◆   ◆

BEING NOBODY: THE CALDRON OF NON-DOING

This next section contains several passages from my journaling over the course of many months. While they are unique to the way I was carried into the dark night of the soul and my manner of individual temperament, they are nevertheless, universal to the process we each go through in dethroning our ego in order to establish a grounding (remembrance) in our deeper authentic Self. I think these passages reflect portals into the odd and confusing ways of Grace in answer to prayer.

JOURNAL ENTRY (BECOMING NOBODY):

What have I embarked upon? What have I started by stating that, "*I see no other reason to live than to be a mystic*?" Does this mean I've now forever stepped into a process that will keep me forever more from "accomplishment" and "recognition" in order that I finally come to simple compassion, love, and service? YIKES! This doesn't suit my personality! (…As if this is even about my personality anyway, GEEEZ, this argument never quits!)

I feel only and continually more lost. More confused. More self-sabotaged. I intellectually accept that my mind can't grasp this, which I seek to know. Yet that's an oxymoron: How can one accept with the mind what one can't know with the mind? So I must not really be accepting anything—at least not with my mind…! (Oh brother!)

So in my body then: What-zup? My legs are tight and muscle bound. I feel tight walking down the stairs. I've run too long without making the time to stretch. I'm starting to stretch (is this a metaphor?) I've had several dreams lately of being in a hazy half-awake state, unable to fully wake up.

I feel sluggish and tired of this process—almost a slight tension at the slowness of it all—like I want the feeling of "AHH! BREAK-THROUGH! but it eludes me still.

Do I have to give up desire as well? It's not even all that strong (obviously—or I'd have at least some motivation to meditate or other things to help me along). It's just a small intention. Maybe I need Bigger desire? Around around around–> again I try and understand with the mind that which the mind can't understand. SO quit. Listen elsewhere! Find a new language...

I feel less than average these days. A nothing nobody. Comparison and loss of what "I could be/should be" leaves its imprint on my days. This is all my ego trying like MAD to regain its stronghold. And even that makes me feel ashamed—"a spiritual failure" even here. It won't stop.

Ego everywhere I turn. I find no other. It dominates. It pokes its head out at every turn. I can find no means to stop its incessant commentary. Can I turn my listening elsewhere? Can I breathe and move from any other point—albeit that I cannot defeat or extinguish this incessant voice? Can another movement carry me nonetheless?

I'm out of my depths. Yet I carry a small (barely visible) thread of faith—a hope that rides on my prayer.

JOURNAL ENTRY (ENDURING NOTHINGNESS):

How DID I get here...? And what does it mean? Is it just accumulated laziness and demolition of will? How do I move from this? I cannot "do" anything. Days and weeks are passing. Months. It's been well over a year of this.

I wander all day. I could fix Steve's website, start a business, create art, volunteer, get another job, clean the house, build a stone walkway, remodel the studio, pick up the trash along the back of the house, empty the truck, clean the sink, develop my manufacturing ideas, do dream analysis, I could meditate. It goes on and on what I could do—and no "thing" gets done!

The tension is grating and tiresome. The fear of some crisis to knock me out of it is great. The sense of futility is everywhere around me. The wish to break through to some spiritual level of understanding is huge.

I read. I run a few miles with Julia. I have dinner and a glass of wine with Steve. That is my day. That has been my day for months and months…

I think I should just start "doing"—doing anything, just to get back into life. But for some reason I cannot. I think I should at least then pray. I cannot. There is not even the desperation to motivate me to pray. Everything is just empty.

How can one endure so much nothing? Why and what is this?

(An artist friend came to our home today to photograph the front entrance door she made for us. Looking around the house at all my ceramic sculpture and art works, she spontaneously said how amazingly talented and alive I am; how my home and everything about me exudes such innovative vibrancy and poetry. I looked at her like a Stepford Wife—and yet I know I have many many gifts.) Why can I not participate in life? Why has everything stopped? I sit and I wander from upstairs and down til bedtime finally again arrives. I sleep 11 hours or more.

Richard tells me to stop running and wander…Shit, his comment must be either projection or undiscerning mentoring. He can't have any idea how much wandering I do. Far more than he's probably ever experienced. I can't stop wandering!

I understand nothing. I remain confused. My existential angst is in its full emptiness. I have no motivation. I seem to wander aimlessly—unable to initiate or participate in any thing.

No sign of let up. No sign of any movement whatsoever.

These first two entries relay a feel for what it was like to continually sit facing no identity. It feels completely empty and horrendous because the experience of not being identified with our careers, our families, our hobbies, our purpose in life, etc., is so foreign to us that it literally feels like a deep caldron of black emptiness.

Facing this state of emptiness is a requisite to finding the fullness of being, that lives and breathes in the place usually taken over by, and filled up with, our self-manufactured identities. We're so tunnel-visioned by our self-constructed identities, that when they are removed, we truly think we are experiencing death. (That is why this process of awakening is often likened to death and rebirth. Again, the paradox: it is, *and* it is not a death. It feels like a death and is met by the ego as one, and in this regard it very much *is* one.)

Experienced as a death to ego (believing that the language of self-identity is what holds us together), it can take quite a battle between the forces of *form* and *undifferentiated consciousness* (or between ego and Soul) before an ear for the musical language of awakening (forever around us) is developed. It truly is learning the sensitivity to an entirely different language; one that comes to see that it is in the still dark emptiness of "no-attachment" that infinite potential lives, breathes, arises to form, and falls back again into undifferentiated consciousness in the great, endless breathing of God.

For months and months I did just this battle—on one level, and then the next: layer after layer after layer in odd confusing spirals. After the obvious battles over loss of external identity (as business woman, artist, athlete) came the more subtle ones: battles over trying to grasp at a "spiritual identity", then (when that was seen through) battles over trying to have a "surrendering identity". If you look into your own process very closely, you'll see the continual attempts to manufacture another identity. And we'll see this again in the journal entry below: "*I'm still hoping for a breakthrough…*"

<u>JOURNAL ENTRY</u> (DESPAIR AND FORMLESSNESS):

I'm still hoping for a "breakthrough" but Steve says I'm getting just what I've asked and prayed for…it just doesn't come the way any of us think it would or should.

All I know is, I feel like I'm too old to start anything (like life's over in a weird way). Can't find any reason to start anything anyway. I'm stuck here in "no man's land". I guess I'm experiencing some degree of death of the ego (or at least perhaps a light is shining on its ever-present masquerade). I do sense that "IT's" all about awareness—not changing anything…or at least not "trying to".

I also see that I am still always running to beliefs out of fear. Even surrendering to life is motivated by fear—like: *"If I can surrender now, perhaps I'll be spared some horrendous crisis forcing me to surrender later."* God, it goes on and on!

I've been living for months, within each day (and within each hour of the day) with the question, *"what shall I do now? And what shall I do now?"*

…So few diversions, that those of my mind-making are filling the screen!

The passage above depicts the circling layers on which the dance between individual identity and formless movement meet and vie for resolve.

The journal entry below is one of those experiences of Grace that come in on the breath of a living prayer. Sometimes we can recognize the grace, often we do not. Here, this night I did, and was cradled in the energetic embrace of Love.

JOURNAL ENTRY (HELD BY GRACE):

Tuesday night I made a CD with Kundun and ending with Barber's Agnus Dei. I did the circular breath process to it for the 50-minute duration, during which I intentionally gave a light focus of intent on the surrendering of my self-will and ego to my inner knowing and to Divine Intelligence. With this, I focused too on the taking down/dismantling of old conditioned responses and habits—as well as on an infusion of faith, healing, and my being/body becoming a clear, open vessel to receive and transmit Divine Intelligence.

During the breathing meditation, I had a most amazing physical and visual perception whereby I saw and felt this kind of "bits and pieces" of fragments pull out from the Ground of Being that was holding me—and then the ground smoothed over in the places where the fragments had come out and dissolved, and the ground became this comforting bed. All night I had a clear, felt sense that my body and being were literally cradled in this large (blue it seems) hand that was the Ground of Being. Too, I could for some time after the meditation, sense back toward Divine Intelligence, and feel a physical opening sensation in the upper region of my head. The feeling of being cradled remained quite strong and direct all night long.

Something jelled this week as I am softly turning my gaze of focus on a unification of my being that is in line with my highest purpose. In the breathing meditation it felt like I was quite clear in offering up a true intention of surrendering my ego and self-will. Some kind of grace has come from this. I pray that my attention remains present and sufficient enough to gain strength and live in the light of this grace. There is a slight kind of "diligence" (a thread of faith) that I now know is required. Within this diligence (this faith) comes grace, and then movement away from conditioning and toward "spontaneous right action" and actual freedom (i.e., real living Presence).

In the above entry, I had, by the grace that comes from a living prayer, been given a glimpse toward freedom. I was beginning to intuit the paradoxical relationship between the essence of faith (or an intended sense of worship), and the element of *non-trying*, non-grasping. The "ego-I" was starting to realize a deeper (out of its control) surrendering into the living Moment of "spontaneous right action" (as Deepak Chopra calls it).

It was when I came to a realization of the hopelessness of it all—i.e., when I came to see that this process couldn't be mastered, couldn't be "achieved" (that I'd still fall into identification, even with "my awakening") that I was finally becoming grounded in the musical language of Source.

This next entry from my journaling perhaps best offers the subtlety of the awakening paradox.

JOURNAL ENTRY (SURRENDERING):

I've become virtually a hermit, removed from almost all the callings of life. No job. No kids. Almost no social interaction. No project— indeed no ability to create/manufacture anything.

These endless, objectless days wouldn't be unpleasant except for the continued nagging guilt and questioning: "Do I lack some important use of will or character and am thereby missing the value/meaning of life? Is this 'doing nothing' just as real and meaningful as any life purpose I could come up with to spend my time? Indeed, is it somehow more valuable (like the quiet time of Thoreau on Walden's Pond)? Is there something 'real' happening to me in this process? Is this a process at all—or is it a hole? Is this part of my evolution? Is there evolution at all? Is it a new language—so completely different from the normal linear rational mind that I miss what is right before me? And if so, how can I willfully intend to discover and learn this unusual language while the only one I know masks its very discovery?…And is there indeed such a subtle language to discover at all?"

Alas, all I can do is hope for some thread of continuing faith in some kind of continuing Grace.

I hope there is a language of the heart. I hope there is an evolutionary (and revolutionary) awakening of the spirit that comes in a gentleness that grows from this stillness.

This is a hard place to sustain. And yet I have no choice in the matter. I remain unable to move, and unable to completely lie back and acquiesce. I've stopped, but the mind has not. I listen as best I can, but I remain unable to discern the subtle incessant tricks of the mind from some deeper and potential messaging of the Soul. I've reached the death of my previous conclusive confidence.

This confrontation of the mind is so terrible to this ego that it tries to annihilate everything around it.

It tries to take down even God: like a warrior who, seeing its entrapment, is determined to only go down by taking his adversary down with him.

◆

I used to relish the strength of my mind. It felt good to use it, to exercise its abilities of insight and perception. I used to believe I had something thereby to offer the world; that the areas of brilliance of my own unique spectrum of consciousness had some purpose and value; that I had something important to offer up to the world.

Now it is all rhetoric. I look at all these teachers and authors and artists and doers of good works, and I see the endless illusions of the ego to fabricate meaning—to overlay and substitute an identity idol as God. The rationalizations are endless. The greedy need of the ego and mind to believe its self-sustaining rhetoric is so strong that the true Grace of Being remains unrealized—or tainted at best (if tainted is better than leaving it alone and unrealized!)

It is hopeless. And I guess that is the truest place to stand.

Acquiescing to the "hopelessness" of my ever truly getting free of this incessant ego, I can certainly go ahead and write, create, "give my unique teaching". But the trap is right here, ever ready to convince me, again and again, that my realizations are whole, that I can express real authenticity, that my voice matters, that my mind is brilliant—that the world needs me! (It grows insidiously like this, until once again the mind has silkily re-mastered its position on the seat of control.)

The fingerprints of the ego are smudged all over the place. Its hand will not ever be fully relinquished. And the myriad ways it will seek to convince us otherwise—to convince us (even) that it has indeed surrendered to a higher source, just so it can remain in its position—is in itself a wonder to behold.

Can anyone ever really embody his enlightened wisdom? And is there transformative evolution at work in the world at all? We continue to cite a mere handful of ancient references (Jesus, Buddha, a few others). Is that the best we've managed all this time, or are there bundles of awakened souls who, because they live embodied in Wisdom, will never be known to us: the true teachers who will never be known as teachers by virtue of their very embodiment?

I want to understand the relationship between a knowing wisdom and the embodied living of it. Or better yet: Forget the understanding of it! I'd like to just live in the embodiment of my knowing wisdom. The "need to understand it" is probably just another barrier.

And so. Here I am. What do I do with this wandering place I am in?

Do I sit mute and in awe? Do I speak it to a soul? Do I write it in a book? Do I stay here unmoved to create, uninvolved in this world? Do I step up and create anyway? I feel no ability to start. I feel no reason to enter. I feebly fight against life—against that "which is" (here, now) but not with any real heart. I am drawn to live within this wandering for as long as it is. And when it is not, I hope to have the faith and courage to live well with what is then.

Who would think it? Who would think that a writing that expresses so many confused questions and such a profound sense of hopelessness could be the movement toward a deep realization that is grounded in freedom? How can hopelessness be a portal into the Fullness of Being? It is so contrary to all the ways we doggedly think, look, listen, and try, that it's no wonder we miss what is forever and always right here!

In this final passage below, this ushering into the Fullness of Being through the subtle portal of paradox is quite stunning. Here, having entered by conscious prayer into the mystic's journey to Soul, and having searched and struggled with the many-headed dragon of illusions, the moment of realization and awakening into the truth of our Being comes through the giving up of the quest! Is that not the ultimate paradox?

Here is the beautiful, universal Homecoming—the returning to a place that was always already right here, in the freedom of surrender.

JOURNAL ENTRY (FREEDOM):

Last night I had my mind blown. I'm not sure what exactly "blew" in my mind, but something.

At the moment I seem to have come to some sort of slight peacefulness about doing nothing/being a nobody. There's nothing to do and no body to be! I still see my guilt and my wish to" figure it all out". And I realize too, that this movement "to figure it out" is itself another fear-based sorry attempt "to appease God by my feigned righteous works" so that I'll be protected and not have to suffer calamities of various horrors; another attempt at control to ease fear via "belief".

I'm thinking it's all a mental fabrication. (Or almost all.) I'm thinking that this world is way beyond any possible understanding vis-à-vis our dualistic constructs. We are probably perpetually caught up in all sorts of rationalizations and interpretations that "explain the meaning of": life, love, God. All these explanations are really just the expression of our built-in addictive drives that are based on survival and driven by fear.

At the moment I seem to be able to relax a little better into life. I can't "get rid of" the fear—it is inevitable. Or, at least "trying" to get rid of it is not the way.

I feel a kind of slight sadness to observe all of humanity's struggling and self-centered efforts to "find IT". It is the wrong search—the wrong quest—the wrong orientation entirely, I feel quite sure.

Maybe like the Chinese finger puzzle, it is necessary for many of us to take this route: to struggle up against the bounds of our minds until we finally exhaust ourselves, experience the limitations, and finally just let go the search for some (non-existent) ending place of ease.

I feel a little depressed (for lack of better word). It may not be depressed, but rather a loosening into a different kind of gentleness that is so unfamiliar as to feel "wrong" somehow.

All I know is the hope for finding inspired meaning is no longer the quest. I've seen too much of its fabricated dangers—and they NEVER cease!

In a way, I feel I'm not looking for something at all any more—except perhaps catching my own focus of attention, and being within conscious awareness as much as I can.

My mind still has some fun postulating and trying to make sense of it all. I suppose it always will. But it is a trap to get caught in that automatic drive, and it's almost like the eye of the needle not to get swept up in our own mental devises, instead keeping centered within the spaciousness of attentive awareness. Of this, I'm now quite certain.

I thought I'd come to "know that I know". I thought that is what transformation would be like. I expected and looked forward to a rosy air of inspiration and delight to wash over me with the realization of conscious unfolding. Well, that's not my experience. I feel an odd quiet that could almost be called resigned, but is something different. More like a freeing.

More like a freeing…Indeed!

9

Knowing I Don't Know

"*Well*" you might be asking just about now:

"How does this story end? How did you return from your journey into the dark night of the soul? How did you find your way back? How did you know it was time to come back at all?"

Excellent questions, all.

I hate to do this to you (again): My answer is steeped to overflowing with seeming paradox. Oddly, in the last entry of my journaling and just before I spontaneously started writing this book, I said:

"I thought I'd come to 'know that I know'. I thought that is what transformation would be like."

What is interesting about this passage are two key things: The reference to the old expectation *"I thought I'd know I know"*, and then, as this is recognized and given up, the stepping into freedom. This small paragraph in fact, summarizes "the whole enchilada", as they say.

Implicit within the stated realization of "not knowing" is a kind of knowing. Can you hear it? I show that I knew I was "done" with my journey, as expressed in reflecting upon the surprise that it didn't resolve in the manner that I thought it would. Herein is a good example of the seemingly paradoxical language of Unity we are called to become sensitized and opened to, in the awakening to *who we really are*. In fact, this is a perfect example.

As long as we keep looking for clues and answers and solutions to life's questions in the same logic stream of our accustomed linear mental functions, we're doomed to missing God's voice. As long as we need to know (in our typical way of "knowing we know"), we will forever miss the more subtle truth. It cannot be attained in this way, but man oh man, are we dogged in our continual efforts to force-fit truth into our self-limiting belief structures! That is, in fact, the key to the mystic's journey in a nutshell: all the force-fitting efforts, structures, belief systems, must be acknowledged for Authentic Relationship (or the honesty of aware participation within each moment) to be lived. It does not mean these ego-identities and structures will no longer exist, just that they cannot be held onto, grasped, or *needed* as the central paradigm of one's existence (that is, if one wishes to find and to know his true Self in Source).

If you wish to know *who you really are*, these self-separating identity structures cannot be the basis on which your living is grounded. As we saw earlier, we create ego-identities in order to establish a sense of self, separate from the Ground of Being. Otherwise, we would remain forever unable to distinguish a difference between "I" and "other". These ego-identities, in a way, establish their own mini-universes—their own definitions of reality. You can see why this has to be so. It's akin to our having skin so we know where our bodies start and stop. As long as we look through the eyes of the self-separating universe of reality, we will forever miss the One that is All.

That is why the journey is necessary: to quiet the noise of the self-separating universe we have created, and in so doing, hear the music of the One that is forever before, around, and within All. When one comes to sit in his Original Nature, which is empty and silent (truly empty and silent), this is what naturally arises: the soft, lilting musical language of all Creation. This language has an intelligence to it which is so much more vast than our own that we find it virtually impossible to hear. And we never will with the mind. The whole Journey to Soul is simply (simply, *ha!*) one of finally finding the original seat of empty silence that is forever before, around, and within all, as the pulsing movement of Life.

To find the Empty Silence, often requires quite a battle with an "ego-king" who is scared to death (literally) to step down from his noise-making theatrical throne. He's not sure that there really is any-One (other than he) to step up and save the kingdom (as in save your soul). He never will know, for the reasons cited above: He exists in and as a separating universe. And therein lies the heart of the struggle. The ego-identity *can never* "know that it knows". It is the wrong instrument entirely. The ego-identity (with its noisy and habituated thought processes and calcified functions of habit that let separateness exist) is in fact, that which blocks the musical language of Unity. It really is a miraculous set-up when you think about it.

The amazing miracle is that there is something else living deeply within us that *can* and *does* know *who we really are*. It is that which is calling us to the Journey of Soul. It is that which we *are* at the very root, before the separation of identity was formed. It is that which created the separation in the first place, so that we could reflect and know Self.

This is why I said earlier and throughout that surrender—i.e., stepping down from that with which we are identified without ever being able to 'know' (in the conventional sense) much less control, that which simply arises as spontaneous creation—is the foundation on which the awakening journey rests.

◆   ◆   ◆

How did I know I had completed my journey?

When my surrender was complete. When I was no longer on a quest. I "looked up" and there simply was no longer a journey. (Reminds me of the old Donovan lyrics: *"first there is a mountain, then there is no mountain, then there is...."*)

I was unwittingly expressing the conclusion of my journey when I wrote in my journal:

> *"I feel I'm not looking for something at all any more—except perhaps catching my own focus of attention, and being within conscious awareness as much as I can."*

I gave up the ghost of "enlightenment", the ghost of something to "get"—the drive to "know I'd know". I even gave up the ghost of surrender. I had come to realize that surrender was never going to be something that is mastered and achieved. It would no longer be surrender if that were the case. One must even come to surrender to the fact that a part of oneself will never want to surrender.

(I know, the paradox again, but it is so!) A part of us will absolutely never be comfortable surrendering. It requires a movement in faith each and every time, moment to moment, throughout our lives. Once this is realized, then comes the paradoxical quality of knowing that which cannot be known.

When one fully sees that there is no final "win": When one sees that the ego-identity will continue to exist and exert its powerful ways—AND yet one knows:

"I Am more than that"—the game is up, the journey is finished. Not finished as in, no more to do; finished as in, one has simply found oneself no longer on a journey. It spontaneously ends when a full surrender to "what is so" has been made. Then surrender becomes a supplicant in the benediction of Faith.

The amazing miracle of it all, is this: Once we heed the call and we take up the mystic's journey, the journey completes itself on the doorstep of each present moment, and how we live it.

Here, is where the real journey lives and continually unfolds. This is where all the action is, right here, right now, in the quality of awareness you and I willingly bring to each moment; in how alive and present to life we are willing to be within each moment. It is a continual question of surrendering into authentic relationship with that *which is.* This is why all the great writings on transformation and enlightenment ultimately come back to something that sounds a lot like: "*Be here now*".

However, to fully understand the deep meaning of "*be here now*" (from the language of Unity in which it is spoken), the journey of undoing must be taken up first. Otherwise we hear with wrong ears, and we practice "*be here now*" as a technique to be learned as opposed to a realization one surrenders into.

This is why "how to" books don't work; why techniques become dogmas; why intellectual understanding without embodied revelation becomes competitive academic mud slinging; why systems of belief become objectified gods in place of the real, living, breathing awareness.

Unless one makes her own inner journey into *coming undone* and falls into her own surrendering of self-identity, no instruction or well-worded wisdom to "*be here now*" can be realized nor truly lived. It is actually more than just "being here now" reflects: It is standing in conscious awareness and intimate relationship with *what is.* One must first be opened and attuned to the language from which this deep realization reverberates and has its meaning, before one can truly realize and surrender into its ways. This is why I chose to write in a vulnerable and personal way that exposes the journey itself. And I pray it may be a worthy companion for your own journey into the soul, whenever and however you are called.

Yes, there surely is a purpose to making the Journey to Soul. It has to be done if we are to live from the awareness of *who we really are.* We are each called to this journey by the deep eternal yearning of God to be known in us. We are called to know the deep Current of Life that is the Source of all that is created. We are called to discover and know ourselves within the musical language of Divine Intelligence. But this journey does not end in the way it began.

I "returned" from my journey of undoing not having achieved the "honored medal of enlightenment", but having discovered that I am called each moment to be born anew in a dynamic and direct relationship with Life. It is a never-ending, moment-by-moment, challenge to live within this differentiated self-identity of form ("I, Ronda"), and yet to participate in life as it presents itself anew within each moment as it arises from the vast spaciousness of the Ground of Being.

We are both *form*, and that which is forever before form. We are the very fluidity of Creation Consciousness taking shape *now* and *now*. I am "Ronda", and *I Am* more than (before the formation of) each congealed form called, "Ronda".

It's truly an awesome challenge! We are called to dance that razor's edge between that which separates us, and that which re-members. Both are needed: Two different universes of reality in a way. The one exists so the other can be seen and known. The ultimate calling (and where I believe evolution is carrying itself) is to become fluid in both languages, simultaneously.

The real story of Soul, is the eternal dance: the Lover and the Beloved who forever embrace and then part, separate and come together in the delight of knowing each other again and anew. This is how Love exists and knows itself.

The Lover calls out to her Beloved in the Great Godly Game of Hide and Seek: *"come out come out wherever you are."* And once again we fall into Her embrace. It is within the living moment that we are forever in the great and eternal dance of Love. Always here, now is the expression of Loving.

◆   ◆   ◆

As I commented in the first part of this book: *"On this journey into the dark night of the soul, one travels blinded, only seeing what one has encountered after it has been well passed by."* This blindness is part of the ungrounding of our habitual ways of knowing, I now realize. It is essential on this journey to come to withstand *"not knowing"*. It is one of the telltale signs of "awakening consciousness", if not the only one: the ability to stand within *not knowing, non-being; identity-less*.

At the time that I made this final journal entry, I did not realize that my journey into the dark night of the soul was ended. I did not see at the time that I wrote those words, these things which I understand and have just brought forth here. In fact, I had absolutely no idea I was going to write this book. No idea what I might have to say! I didn't "plan" to write this chapter either. I literally mistyped the chapter starting the next section as Chapter 10 when I realized there was no Chapter 9. And so I opened a page and wrote what may be the most important part of this writing. This too is part of the exquisite beauty and mystery of it all.

Remembering is a free-fall into Faith. It is surrendering into the living moment—and the joy in letting life continually offer up her mysterious surprises. Life will always bring surprise when we give up the reigns of control and the very small box such control requires. There is a language of the heart that we all have available to us: It is the voice of Divine Intelligence. It is the musical language of Love itself. When we open to this Divinely Intelligent music of Love, the miraculous naturally and spontaneously occurs.

It is from that openness that these very words flow here, now. Not *"my"* words, but those of Life coming through this one unique reflection called *"Ronda"*. To the extent that you and I are able to *let* drop our own controlling ways, can the language of Love speak through each one of us—each with a unique spectrum of illumination. What an amazing turn of events! The individual isn't denied or sacrificed in this process of awakening, rather he is elevated into the highest service to Life: the Communion of Love.

This is what we are each called to know: the celebration and joy of living as worship, of living as Love expressed in the dance of the Lover and her Beloved.

This is the One Story. The Story we are each called to live and to tell. And we tell this story within our *presence of Being—in Love.*

Now the storytelling journey is yours...

Poem/Prayer: The Calling

(Part II. At The Dawning)

Long have I slept
Tucked in your blanketed vigil;
Rapt in your Presence and Grace.

When somewhere near dawning,
My Beloved,
You reach out to touch my face.

With idyll caress your fingertips
Travel the contours and crevasses of my yearning.
My field of dreams
They each flower and blush
At your greedy and tender seeking.

Your hand grazes my shape,
Memorizing each curve and each sighing:

> The fullness of my belly,
> The swelling at my breast.
> You know each breath
> Before
> It rises and recedes again from my lips;
> Each fancy before I've given it notice.

You've known me before I've known myself!
You've spoken my name;
Called me out of the dark skies
Of impermanence:
Spilling my tears into the Nameless One.

I am painted across the skies of impermanence.

And I know who I am.
...I know who I am!

PART III
A Companion Guide...

10

Living Your Destiny

○ ○

"A man is what his deep, driving desire is.
As his deep driving desire, so is his will.
As his will is, so is his deed.
As his deed, so is his destiny."

—*Translation of Katha Upanishad from*
Dialogue with Death by Eknath Easwaran.

What is the meaning of life? What am I here to express? How do I find my soul's purpose? What is my destiny? How do I know that I'm on the right path?...Or if I'm not on the right path, how do I get there?

These are the kinds of questions all of us ask and grapple with, at least on occasion. They are the kinds of questions that stir up all sorts of books and seminars, therapies and practices. We each have that built in "dissatisfaction factor" stimulated by an inner yearning. Some part of each of us wants very much to know and to fully be able to express our own unique reflection of God-consciousness. Somewhere *in there* we know that this is ultimately why we are here. Somewhere deep inside we sense that there is a sacred and unique purpose to our lives. Often times for most of us, we only know this feeling as a small, wishful hope that we hardly dare express: *"Could it possibly be that I have a unique destiny—a purpose for my life?"* Still it is there, even as a small thread of hope: *"What do I live for? What is my purpose?"*

As I said at the very beginning of this book, these are sacred questions. They are the awakening questions. They live and move and well up from deep within our souls. These questions are the calling of our hearts to remember who we really are.

These questions frame a good place upon which to focus the start of one's Journey to Soul. It is good to ask them, to grapple with them, to deeply question yourself. These questions contain the power of your soul within them because they spring from your soul's yearning. The depth to which you engage yourself within these sacred questions will be the depth to which you will be brought to meet and to know your soul's purpose. Really it is that plain and simple.

We each have layer upon layer of unfolding inner awareness and awakening to know and express. And life constantly reflects back to us the level of awareness we are willing to know. The intent behind our living is a constant living prayer, and it is constantly met and given back. This is perhaps difficult to take in. But I've come to see it very directly. Each of us sends a message to life all the time in the form of our choices, our beliefs, our fears, and in the extent of our willingness to be open to life. These messages are literally the deeper meaning of prayer. They *are* prayer.

Problem is, we're not always really clear with where we stand. We're not clear as to what message we are sending. This is where and why the Journey to Soul comes into play: to meet our various contradictory voices, and synchronize to our deepest soul's intent.

We all have subconscious and automatic belief systems that are transmitted into life—and heard as prayer. For example, let's say that I believe that I truly want to awaken to my highest purpose; to God's calling as expressed through me. I may compose a prayer asking for this, I might attend workshops on living my soul's purpose, I may read books and do their exercises to help me know and express my soul's purpose. All these conscious efforts are confirming *"yes, I want to know and express my soul's deepest purpose."*

But meanwhile and simultaneously, there are inner fears, hesitancies, and control issues that I am not fully aware of having, simply because they are the very fabric of my self-identified structure of reality. Can you get a glimpse of this? On the outer surface I may genuinely believe I am saying "yes" to life and to manifesting my soul's purpose. (I may even be moved to tears of rage and frustration, to deep yearning despair, in my longing for living my soul's purpose.) But as long as this desire for the expression of my soul's deep purpose is encased in the subconscious fears of my protective ego-identity-structure, I am simultaneously sending out a very strong subliminal "no" to that very prayerful intent. I am, in actuality, sending contradictory messages.

It goes even deeper than this. Matters of soul and the expression of our God-consciousness cannot express themselves fully within the limiting confines of the protected ego-reality. Soul is much larger than, and prior to, these ego-identity-structures that we create as part of becoming functioning individuals, separate from the undifferentiated Ground of Being. To fully know and to express one's deepest authenticity, one must be willing to meet soul outside of the ego-structure. And this means getting clear about one's subconscious messages. It means really taking a good deep look at your soul's yearning and then getting honest about the limits and "stops" you, yourself, impose by way of the fear and refusal to free-fall into Grace.

For me, and out of my soul's deep yearning, I asked myself this question:

"What really matters in life?"

When you really stop and think about this question, a lot comes up. For one thing: what else is there to ask of ourselves than the question of what really most matters in life? And once that question is sincerely posed, well, to quote a phrase, "all hell breaks lose!"

I took up the question as a quest (which it is). I dialogued with it, I meditated on it, read books that stimulated my thinking until I found my own inner answering unfold within me.

I came to see that very few things really matter against the backdrop of our own mortality and the quickness of life. I came to see, in fact, that all that really matters is my fundamental relationship to life as the movement of God.

I came to rephrase my quest by asking myself this further question:

"How alive do I dare be in each moment of communion with life?"

For me, this became a very serious quest. "How alive do I truly dare to be in this life? Can I bear being fully present to my own and others' suffering? Can I bear to abide in the moments of painful relationship? Can I be truly present for the full range of life: for anger, for love, for boredom, for embarrassment, for failure, for joy, for sadness, for disease, for death? Can I really stop hiding behind the façade of control, and fall into an unconditional relationship with Life and whatever it brings me? Can I let Life live through me freely, without ducking for cover behind almost countless numbing strategies?"

Upon asking these questions, I started to notice all the ways I contradict myself: the ways I hide from life, keep it at arm's distance, deny my full presence to Life *as it is* before me, here, now. In short, I started to see all the ways I was unconsciously saying "no" to that which I believed to be "yes". There are hundreds of them. We all have them. They exist within the territory of our self-cre-ated identity structures that (we believe) hold us together as separate beings. They are the mechanisms of "how we forget" as discussed in Chapter three. In fact, all the myriad ways we hide from being fully present to life have as their basis the primordial fear of non-existence. Our subconscious "no's" to living soulfully are a reflection of the ego-king's absolute terror of stepping down from the throne and being beheaded.

Everything that is constructed for the sake of feeling secure (belief systems, habitual ways of responding, personality characteristics, things that make us feel we are in control) are the ways we say "no" to authentic relationship to Life ever new each moment. They are the ways that we sacrifice true aliveness for habitu-ated illusions of security. We literally "buy ourselves" the illusion of security at the cost of our soul's living expression. Simple as that I'm afraid.

When I started seeing, layer after layer, all the ways I say "no" to Life: the numbing of wine, my attachment to being right, using exercise to "run from", preparing my rebuttal instead of really listening to what the person beside me is trying to express, judging, feeling "better than" or victimized, covering up with chatter that which is trying to come through silence, and on and on—when all these "no's" start to parade before the mind's eye, the full ramification of the quest becomes deeper. When one starts to awaken to the contradictory messages she is giving to life, true Authenticity has started to creep in and take over the seat of power.

And so now I ask you: "*How alive do you really dare to be?*"

How much "yes" can you give to life, really and truly? How many fearful "no's" can you give up for a true "yes"? That is the calling of Soul for each of us, each and every moment of our lives!

If you look deeply and honestly into this quest, you'll start to see unraveling all the thousands upon thousands of ways you, I, and our society, continue to do almost anything but be truly alive and present to the moment. In fact, it is the rare moment that we are truly alive and present. Those are the moments of enlightenment. (Yet we try so hard to find "enlightenment" by any other means than by truly offering ourselves in simple presence to Life…)

It comes down to this: We live most of the time "out of sync", in a state of contradiction. On the one hand, we sense the longing of our Soul's desire. And on the other hand, we feel the physical ego-identity's needs to be in control. This is precisely why one is called eventually to take the Journey to Soul. Without this journey into an "undoing" of the ego-identity, we merely force-fit Soul into a very limited expression of our self-contained ego-reality.

Sooner or later, the eternal yearning is not content within this controlled environment, and we are called to a fundamental undoing of self-identity in order to freely meet and come to know our Authentic Selfhood within the unconditional Living Presence. When this impetus occurs, Grace has descended—and one is ushered into "undoing", surrender, and re-awakening into the language of Unity.

There is an essential surrender that is required of all who come to remembering who they really are. It is required because it is implicit to the very process of re-membering. Essential to awakening into the Fullness of our Being—to our soul's deepest purpose—is meeting, and not running from the innate primordial fear of non-being that is at the very root of our self-identity (with all of its many masks to control and contain that fear, including our belief systems, hiding techniques, diversions, self-righteous opinions, and on and on it goes). We have to meet—and know—these fears in order to become "more than they". Otherwise, we live within fear's domain and we are limited by fear's controls.

There's a paradoxical twist in all of this (naturally), and it is important. Awakening to our soul's expression requires not only the willingness to meet our deep unconscious fears (and the many masks they hide behind), but it requires a kind of honoring of these fears in an odd way. We come to realize we are hopeless before them, and yet, by being able to recognize them, we are clearly *more than* these fears. In the honest, "eyes wide open" acknowledgement of our helplessness to control or master fear, a surrendering has been spontaneously offered. It is by this very open willingness to look at, know, and feel the fear, that you are freed from its grips. Not that it goes away. The mechanisms of fear never go away. Rather, by seeing how the fear continually tries to stop you, and by opening and surrendering into Life anyway, you come to realize/remember that Essential Self who lives, rests, and has her being in the unconditional fullness of Unity.

I hope you see that we do not transcend—as in master or rise above our fears. Rather, by no longer fighting against them in inexhaustible ways, we are spontaneously and naturally released into a deeper wellspring of Freedom; released into the realization of Essential Being that exists forever before and beyond ego self-identification.

I hope you see why this is not a one-time movement of conscious awakening, but a life-long/evolution-long continual process of coming to stand before Life, and in awareness of the fear-driven "no's", to consciously offer up a resounding "Yes". This is what we are asked forever in the Eternal Now: to stand, knowing the power and strength of that which seeks to say "no" inside each of us, and to willingly acknowledge the "yes" that is prior to and *more than* the no. Not to conquer, banish, or kill the "no's", but to acknowledge them openly and willingly within an awareness of the pre-existing "yes".

It is part of our calling within the Great Godly Game of Hide and Seek: to hide and to seek; to find and to forget. We are called to live within these physical bodies and their separating structures, and yet we are asked also, to remember and to know *who we are* as the Creator of this structural separation of form and reflection. It is an awesome calling! It is literally a never-ending, moment-by-moment dance in the great breathing of God.

◆　　◆　　◆

Enough of the lay of the land, I want to offer some practical applications for finding and expressing your soul's purpose in life. So for starters, how can one initiate a Soul Quest?

INITIATING A QUEST:

The Journey to Soul begins by initiating a quest. A quest is initiated by the posing of deep, inner questions. The question (not the answer) is the seed of awakening.

Ask yourself one or more of these questions (they essentially are asking the same thing using different words, so pick whichever you feel more drawn to).

What really matters?
What is my soul's purpose?
What is my life for?
To what do I dedicate my life's meaning?

Spend some time with the question (like weeks, months even). Journal, read, meditate on what comes up for you as you ponder your question. Go as deeply as you can into the question, and what it means in your life.

When you find yourself with answers to the question (or with further, deeper questions), dialogue with these: meditate on them, do some automatic writing, see how far you can let these questions or answers take you into deeper terrain.

Below are a few send-off questions to take you deeper into your Soul Quest. But please, don't see this as a quick exercise to take from a book and move on. Sit with these exercises a while; let the intent of your quest mull around in your being.

In fact, this is my first send-off suggestion: I strongly urge you to decide that you're going to keep posing your basic questions as a kind of living, evolving mantra (as indeed they are). Then, like in meditation, observe where the continual posing of the question leads…

Ask:

- *Where in my life do I already express the qualities of my life's deepest purpose?*

- *What holds me back from greater expression?* (As much as you can, take this question inward to discover your own inner blocks, fears, beliefs—the "no's" you utter—rather than externalizing to outer circumstances or other people you feel hold you back. The latter is rarely (ultimately, never) true.

- *How deep is my desire to live my soul's purpose?* A good way to question yourself deeply is to ask the following "Dreaded Give-Up Questions".

"THE DREADED GIVE-UP QUESTIONS":

How much are you willing to give up (if you had to) in order to know and live your soul's purpose?…Are you willing to give up your home? Your relationship? Your family? Your health? Are you willing to give up financial security? Career identity? Are you willing to give up your various comforts and attachments? Are you willing to give up your various addictions or distractions (caffeine, alcohol, TV, sex, sports, sleep)?

I know I know! You're saying, *"This is stupid. Why should I have to give up these things to find my soul's purpose? That's ridiculous."*

Ask the questions anyway!

You know why? Because right here, in all of these things we don't want to give up, is where we find the deep-seated fears that are continually sending out the message of "no", and drowning out our appeals for "yes" in the yearning desire to remember and live our soul's intent.

Right here, in these exact questions, will you find your contradictions of intent. You will be led (as I was) to question the depth of your desire for soul; you will start to meet and discover the fear of non-being, and the ceaseless antics of the "ego-king" with his various masks and clever tricks to try and keep you away from the threatening region of Soul.

Asking these questions, and following the course of your answering, will unravel the whole intricate maze that forever seeks to keep us contained (safe and sound) within the structures of self-identity. We don't want to ask ourselves these questions. We're deathly afraid of asking them. But ask yourself: "*who's afraid?*" It is the separating ego-identity that we have constructed, and then come to identify as the very source of "me", that is afraid. We are more than these separating identities, but we have forgotten by way of over-identification with these separate ego-identity-structures. (This is why the clever ego says, "*This is stupid!*")

Ask the questions anyway. I tell you, this is the very seed of awakening. It is right here, in the asking, that we begin to realize we are "more than", just by the simple act of acknowledging the part that is not wanting to ask—and "asking anyway". It is here that we start to hear and attune to the musical language of Unity; here that we start to meet and sense the Fullness of our Being.

Amazing, but so: We find the true abiding light of ourselves by entering the dark pathways of fear and avoidance. So, like the Nike™ advertisement, I say to you: "*Just do it!*" By daring to ask, you will have made the essential leap into remembering who you really are.

MAKING THE ACT OF LIVING PRAYER:

What is your destiny?...

I've always felt a bit confused about the notion of destiny. Is it fate? Is it something I can miss or refuse? Is it just, "*Que sera sera; whatever will be, will be*"?

I heard this word "destiny" with new insight as I 'came across it in a book I was reading by Eknath Easwaran quoting from the Katha Upanishad, in his book entitled, *Dialogue With Death* (probably not a best-seller by way of title alone, but a very good book on the mystic's journey). I'll write it again:

> "*A man is what his deep, driving desire is.*
> *As his deep driving desire, so is his will.*
> *As his will is, so is his deed.*
> *As his deed, so is his destiny.*"

I've come to see that destiny is stirred awake by our deep desires, and then lived within our deeds as we live each moment. This is why if we have contradictory desires (like, "I want to live my soul's purpose, *and* I want to keep my ego happy and secure"), we will experience a contradictory destiny. This is why it is good to continually pose these questions I suggest, and to become as clear as we can with the desires fueling our deeds.

I've come to see that the living of destiny is what I call our *living prayer*. It is by way of our deepest desires that we are constantly praying all the time:

"*In the beginning was the word....*" (In the beginning of what is to be created, is our desire, our intent.)

"*And the word was made flesh....*" (And our desires fueled our actions and our choices.)

"*And dwelt among us.*" (And fulfilled themselves as destiny—as our experience.)

We can look at our lives each moment, and notice that which we are living as our destiny. So the personal question becomes: "*What are you praying for, really praying for—i.e., what is your most essential living desire or sense of purpose?*" And, "*What other desires are you willing to sacrifice, give up, to fulfill the living of this deepest purpose, your destiny?*" It doesn't mean that you *must* start giving these things up. It means (if you truly want to open to your own remembering) that you must become clear about what prayers you are uttering, and the bounds and contradictions of these prayers.

OFFERING A LIVING PRAYER:

Throughout this book I've made references to the offering up of what I call a "*Living Prayer*". A living prayer is more than the typical notions of prayer where we appeal to God "out there", spilling out our personal concerns, our appeal for help, and our gratitude. These are prayers of petition and thanksgiving, and not true Living Prayer. What I mean by a "living prayer" is the more organic, deep prayer that arises non-verbally, even before words. It is that which we deeply yearn for, feel communion with, worship as the very celebration of Life in us. A living prayer is connected and alive to the mysterious feeling of Presence.

Most of the time when we pray—while it may be very genuinely felt and deeply delivered—it is still not fully connected and in alignment within one's deepest truth. There are too many other competing desires and interests that we are scarcely (if at all) aware of, and they block (or interrupt) the connection. Actually, we're issuing living prayer all the time; it's just that we don't realize the mixed messages that get carried along within the Soul's deeper intent. Our living prayers—with the mixed messages that tag along—send out the call for each and all of these contradictory desires to be delivered as destiny.

Everything we do is the issuing of a prayer. Everything starts by prayer (*"in the beginning was the word"*). Everything comes into being from prayer. So yes, it is true: "Be careful what you ask for." I'd take it another step: *Become aware of what you ask for unconsciously.* As we increase our awareness, by daring to ask the questions that take us into regions the ego-identity does not want us to go, we will naturally come to live in ways that are less contradictory and more synchronized with our conscious desires. We will become more fully available to our deepest essence. And, this is a life-long quest.

When we enter the Quest of the Soul and we dive into the questions posed above, then a more conscious and attuned living prayer may be invoked. This is what I offered as an example in Chapter five of the prayer-song that was created consciously within the initiation of my quest. The honest *eyes wide openness* of that prayer made it a more unified living prayer than I had issued in my life previously. And as a result, it was answered with a much more profound and powerful deepening of my awakening into the Fullness of Being. Another way of looking at it is, I had more consciously invoked my destiny.

A PRACTICAL INSTRUCTION IN LIVING PRAYER:

I don't know about you, but for many years I shied away from the notion of prayer. I definitely wouldn't use the word "prayer" aloud or in conversation with friends. It was somehow too childish or too outside of oneself. I guess my difficulty with prayer came from an old hang-up stemming from my early church training, and the image of some wizened and white-haired man up in heaven listening for our prayers.

I went through my more *chic* new-age affirmation phase too; offering up empowered mini-manifestos as a mini-god/creator. There is obviously truth, and certainly power, behind the use of affirmations. But for me, the approach started to feel a little too ego-manipulated—a little too control-based in its driving agenda, as opposed to being an offering and surrendering of the heart to the Source of all Creation in which we are already seated.

I've come back to using the word "prayer" because, for me, it implies an *offering up*. It implies a humbling of oneself in reference to that which is forever larger than the ego-controlled "me". I believe the humbling act of *offering up* is, in itself, an essential, invoking agent of prayer. It is being willing to step outside of our self-identification structure (and its wishes and desires for control), and enter into the greater mystery of an unknowing, dynamic aliveness. This is the liberated free-fall into the wellspring of Creation, where all things that are made, come in to being, in what Deepak Chopra calls "the black void of infinite and pure potential".

A SUGGESTION FOR LIVING PRAYER:

What am I suggesting to you in all of this? I am suggesting that you make conscious *living prayer* a fundamental part of your life. Not a bunch of *little prayers* made "for this" and "to have that". Let those go for a while if you can. Instead, what I mean by making conscious prayer a fundamental part of your life, is taking up this quest—taking up these questions you are posing to yourself—and offering them up as a conscious prayer. Keep your prayers focused on your quest.

Create prayers that come as close as you can to expressing the clarity and depth of living your Soul's Purpose. In fact, you might not even consider what I'm suggesting a prayer at all. That's good! In fact, it might be helpful actually to consider it more like creating a poem that expresses, in loving terms, that which you have come to see and to know thus far on the quest of your Soul. As your clarity deepens from your first Living Prayer, offer up a deepened prayer that reflects your newest depth of *felt understanding*. This kind of fundamental prayer is the very seed of awakening. It will carry you always closer to your True Nature.

Be as clear as you can in the energy/feel of your Living Prayer. When we butt up against the tricks of the ego, all sorts of confusions, fears, and way-laying messages like, *"this is just a stupid waste of time"* will come in. Don't focus your prayers on "getting rid of" or overcoming these tricksters. That merely gives these fearful parts of ourselves more stay-power by way of the energy we give to *fighting against* them or trying to be *released from* them. Pray instead toward the depth of what you sense/know as the higher Truth. Acknowledge your fears and mind-tricks in your prayer, but not as an appeal to have them taken away. Rather, offer a prayer toward faith within fear, wisdom within confusion; toward the feeling of your deepest yearning.

As beautiful and powerful as the sacred prayers of saints and sages are, I'm suggesting here that you find your own truest voice for expressing that which you sense right now of your awakening journey. Speak from what you know as truth at this time. Make this your prayer. Try to see how close you can come to what you "feel as truth" at this moment. When you find that closeness, there will be an inner feeling of *"Yes, this speaks with vibrancy to that which I sense as my deepest truth in this moment."* That is the voice of a living prayer. And a living prayer always, always, carries you ever closer to the Truth of your Soul.

SUMMARY OF PRACTICAL SUGGESTIONS:

1. Initiate the Soul Quest: *"To what do I dedicate my life's meaning?*

2. Pose the Quest as a meditation mantra, and follow the thoughts and feelings that arise.

3. Discover and acknowledge your contradictory desires (your "no's" to Soul) by asking *"The Dreaded Give-Up Questions".*

4. Offer up a conscious *living prayer*—i.e., one that comes as close as you can possibly get to expressing the clarity and depth of your understanding, and of your intent (including acknowledgement of "the good, the bad, and the ugly").

5. Consecrate your Prayer by making it a living mantra (a living focus) around which your life is blessed and your awareness is attuned.

11

A Compass for the Dark

In a way, I feel this entire book has been written to serve the intent of this one chapter: to provide a compass for the dark and slippery terrain one eventually must meet on this Journey to Soul. Everything I've expressed and shared, including several of my own direct experiences and revelations within the process of *remembering who I (really) Am*, has been offered to cast some guiding light onto a precarious terrain.

In particular, I hope I have demystified the treachery of coming to meet what is commonly called "the dark night of the soul". I hope you have come to see more clearly that this treachery is not some mystical rite of passage created by a large mythic and sadistic gate-keeper who holds prisoner your very soul, but rather, the natural barriers constructed by the ego (as its own universe) in order to do well its job of creating and maintaining self-separation. It *is* still a mystical rite of passage. It's just that it is we, ourselves, who have become overly identified with the universe of our ego-identities, thereby forgetting *who we really are* before these self-identity universes were created.

It reminds me of the old Pogo quote by Walt Kelly, "*We have met the enemy and he is us!*" (It has the ring of truth about it.)

◆   ◆   ◆

As highlighted in Chapter three, we all get lost *in* ourselves and thereby we are lost *from* our Authentic Self. We all forget, through the process of individuation, *who we are* at the root of our Being, before these ego-defined identity structures were created and we moved into them (more or less) full time. The primordial survival instinct is so inherent to life! Is it any wonder this same instinct is brought to bear by an ego that is merely intent upon protecting its universe? The bigger wonder to me is that we are called to supercede such a strong and basic instinct, in order to remember that which existed (and exists) *before* the individual "I" was constructed, characterized, and conditioned. No wonder in the great mythic stories, this journey to remembering is called the "Hero's Journey". No wonder in the sacred and mystical texts of the world's religions, this journey is referred to as a death and rebirth.

The kind of overthrow that is required of all that we stake our identity and security upon is truly an epic undertaking. Who knows how many thousands upon thousands of years human consciousness must evolve before it is able to make this kind of leap at all.... Who knows what the next leap—in an endless array of consciousness unfolding—will require? It is truly a mind-boggling and fantastic journey! And this brings me back to the subject of the mind, and its continual "boggling".

You know the "sadistic gatekeeper" I said doesn't exist? Well, in a way she does: she is your very own ego-intelligence, your clever mind-control. The entire process of the Journey to Soul—coming to surrender our over-identification with the *ego-king,* and thereby free-fall into *the remembering of who we really are*—is one mammoth chess match for the mind. And the mind *hates* to lose! (Very poor sport, actually.)

The biggest (really the only) threat and treachery in the journey of awakening, is meeting and rising above the tricks of the mind to try and keep you right here in the safety net of your ego-structured universe. You have to go in and do battle with what you consider to be *you.* UGH! *(Go figure!)*

I don't know that words can well express the subtlety with which the mind can, and will, throw up every kind of trick imaginable (and many more that are unimaginable) just to keep itself seated at the throne of its self-created universe; I've tried, in many ways, to give you a glimpse by way of my own confusions, loss of confidence, sense of failure. The ego-mind will even try (as one more in an endless repertoire of clever moves) to pretend and convince you that it *is* your very Soul. (And *ohhhh,* so deep and sensitive a soul it claims to be, too!) The masquerading play-acts and antics of the mind is nothing short of stellar. (*Hearty applause in recognition.*)

FINDING GUIDING LIGHTS:

What I truly know is this: You *will not* catch all the mind-tricks you play on yourself. You're too much inside the maneuver to see them clearly. You *will* become caught in them. We all do. In fact this is the one place a teacher or a guide is really important. Not someone who will lead you through the briars and brambles—only you can do that, as it must be done alone and for oneself—but someone who will help point them out, so you will see: *"Oh this is a briar, not the truth like I thought…. In fact it's rather prickly in here."*

Throughout all the mystical writings concerned with matters of transformation and enlightenment, there is a realized call for a teacher or guide, simply because the very thing we are called to see is outside of the eyes with which we have become conditioned to see. (We have to get out of the box before we can see that we were in one!) A teacher or guide is needed because it is truly an epic journey. It's more than a major, life event. It is an evolutionary leap of (God knows) how many millions of years in the making.

We are called to willingly hand down the very thing we believe keeps us alive. The process of transcending the limited self-separating identity is literally met as a death experience. And as such, the lengths to which the mind will go to keep us from that feared death, is absurdly impressive and virtually endless. This is precisely why the *living prayer* is so essential. Living prayer is the portal that leads beyond self-identification. It creates a crack in our self-created castle walls.

For myself, I discovered a composite of guides that are helpful along this epic path. I share the main ones with you by way of giving you a few ideas for yourself.

BOOKS:

Books are great guides. We have such easy access to all the world's great writing, not only the traditional religious stories and parables that reflect this timeless Journey of Awakening, but so many new, deepening interpretations on these classical works. I have always been a big reader in the areas of religion, metaphysics, mysticism, and evolution of consciousness. I read a very diverse repertoire of authors, and I read a lot. I read to remember and to contemplate. I never take someone's word as truth unless it tastes as such on my own lips. I let the "strange coincidences" guide my reading: a book that falls into my hand; a page that I open at random; a title I feel called toward; a book someone spontaneously mentions. I follow endless trails on Amazon.com! By no means extensive, by no means complete (and realizing I'll likely have two or three more that I will wish to add as soon as this book is printed) I have nonetheless offered in the appendix, a list of those books I've found of particular impact.

Of particular emphasis, I'd like to highlight the book by John Welwood, *Toward A Psychology Of Awakening: Buddhism, Psychotherapy, and the Path of Personal and Spiritual Transformation.* This work is, to date, the most profound and masterful synthesis I've ever encountered for integrating Western psychological mind and understanding with Eastern spiritual realization. It very clearly expresses an integrated framework for coming to a true wholesomeness of Being. If you select only a couple books from my list, I have to hope this is one.

ABIDING FRIENDSHIPS:

Friends and loved ones, who share at least a basic understanding of psycho-spiritual dynamics and/or who are attuned within their own hearts to a life of conscious awareness, offer great day-to-day mirrors reflecting movement and growth. Be careful though to allow for friends and loved ones who may balk at, or be threatened by, your inner challenges and changes. Keep a clear eye out for those who can attune to the subtlety and fluidity that your quest requires, and let the others re-discover the you that is emerging, if or as they can. This requires a subtle acceptance of "*what is*", which is the only way one can truly allow for change to emerge. For me, my husband and sister are excellent guides because they, too, have made their own journeys and understand deeply (if not my ways) the often confusing and contradictory terrain common to all.

"COINCIDENCE" AND SPONTANEITY:

Learning to listen in new or different ways from those normal to you, provides excellent potential for a guiding light. The process of opening to our true Authenticity requires giving up old habituated ways of "knowing", and instead learning new and subtle ways of seeing. Everything you can do to help let go of old patterns and open to new ones helps this process. For example, watching for seeming coincidences, things that are oddly related; keeping your ears attuned to repeated patterns; learning to listen in ways in which you are unaccustomed—all these help break down automatic, habituated responses and attune you to messages you've missed because of these habits. If you are intellectually oriented (as I am) try learning to listen more to the intelligence of your body and your heart. Imagine being able to understand the speaking of nature, the language of trees.

DREAM WORK:

Our dreams, if we allow them, are a constant, running commentary on "the state of our Union", a pointing to the briars that block our way, and an illumination on the heart and soul of our own deep Being. Dreams are the Soul's way of talking to us each night. For many (if not most of us), interpreting our dreams is very difficult. They seem often to be so illogical, bizarre, and sometimes frightening or confronting. The key is to learn the language of symbol and metaphor. Nothing is necessarily what it seems. A dream of your son being killed can be symbolic of "a boy part of you" that is being "cut off or denied". It takes quite a good deal of "getting out of oneself" in order to look at a dream and reap its deeper language of meaning. There are many good books and workshops on dream work. In particular, stay with someone who guides you to finding your own meaning, and avoid any who interpret for you or give canned meanings of symbols. Sexual dreams may be a spiritual commentary. Spiritual images may be making commentary on physical health issues. But nothing is for sure. You have to learn to dialogue with them yourself. It is endlessly fascinating and rich ground for inner awakening.

"EXPERTS" (THERAPISTS, GURUS, MINISTERS AND SELF-REALIZATION TEACHERS):

Beware! (How's that for my first suggestion?) I make it right off the top because, it seems to me, so many of us tend toward looking to others for what we need to find within ourselves. So many of us give ourselves away to experts and "how-to" strategies. Workshops, therapies, and working directly with someone who considers himself a spiritual teacher can obviously be very helpful, but it is also potentially dangerous ground. This path is the traditional one, and it requires the utmost in personal responsibility and vigilance. If you take this path, be sure to only work with someone who truly speaks to your heart's deepest wisdom. I spoke earlier about the miracle of finding a teacher in Chapter five, and that section I believe speaks well for how to wisely enter this kind of a relationship.

BODY AWARENESS AND HEALTH:

Body awareness and health of the body is really important. For one thing, the territory you are entering on the Quest of Soul is so potentially confused and contorted, that a healthy body helps keep a clear and calm presence for the intensity of the journey. Also though (and perhaps more important) is the intelligence that only the body can speak. The body has a connected intelligence with all of life and living that is much more pure and accurate than the overlays of the emotions and the mind. If you really want to know your deepest truth, learn the language of your body intelligence by keeping it fit and staying tuned to its speaking. (An excellent book noted in the appendix, entitled, *Bio-Spirituality*, by Peter A. Campbell and Edwin M. McMahon, speaks with great clarity to the body's inherent spiritual intelligence. I highly recommend reading it.)

LIVING PRAYER:

Prayer is actually the very essence of this journey as highlighted in the previous chapter. My own living prayer has consistently been my strongest guiding light. It shines from the deepest place within myself that is calling me Home. By the grace of my living prayer, I am continually led to guides and teachers and revelations, as I need them.

MEDITATION:

I believe meditation is one of today's most misunderstood and misused practices. Too often it has become the effort of "stopping thought", or the desire/addiction for "entering bliss". So I suggest merely this: experience simply sitting and doing nothing, not "trying to", or "trying *not* to" do anything, not worrying about posture or hand placement or breath, or stillness or emptiness. Simply sitting and being with whatever *is*.

Be bored. Be anxious. Be busy. Be any or all of these things. And see, "*who is it that is these things?*" In my experience, it is simply in the *doing of* this, that the power and the point of meditation is realized. Meditation can be used for providing stress reduction, entering a state of peace or bliss, and gaining contemplative insights. However, the ultimate and genuine purpose of meditation is to help see and sustain that same, simple willingness to be present to *whatever is* within the regular moments of living (be it washing the dishes, arguing with a friend, or writing a report). Meditation is the continual re-membering to ask, "*can I say yes to what life is presenting me in this moment, by being fully present to it?*" It is a simple re-issuing (and awakening) of one's willingness to be present to Life. And this is a forever in-the-moment challenge within a ceaseless evolution of remembering.

USE OF A SPIRITUAL PRACTICE:

Spiritual practice as a focus of intent (or a *living prayer*) certainly has an elemental force in awakening to *who we really are*. But eventually the focus must shift from *practice* to *being*. That is, whatever one uses as a spiritual practice, must eventually stop being looked upon and treated as "a discipline" or "a method". Rather, it must become an integrated aspect of how one naturally and organically moves, breathes, and expresses these energies as the inevitable and integral reflection of simply living within the dynamic freedom of one's True Nature.

In fact, the only genuinely deep purpose for any spiritual practice is to simply come to know and embody its essence as the natural and spontaneous communion with Life itself. This is our natural birthright.

To first *sample* our natural birthright (and even discipline it as a practice) offers the energetic of a *remembering resonance* within the seed of our heart's deepest desire to awaken. What I see that really saddens me, however, is that these various spiritual disciplines can be (and often are) "technically practiced" and "efforted" by many people for years and still never "known" as the embodiment and unfolding of a Living Presence. This control-based tendency for dogmatic discipline and a desire for mastery often becomes yet another trap.

I've discovered that in order to *know* a spiritual practice as the expressed embodiment of Authentic Being, it must be "listened into" until something *in the voice of the practice* is heard within one's body. And once this voice is truly heard, and the voice is followed as the course of movement for one's response, this particular practice or method will naturally open the person into attunement (atonement) as Living Essence. That is the hidden secret and power behind spiritual practice. It is the secret and power behind all true expressions of creativity.

I believe that spiritual practices are a *Calling* initially; a calling to the musical language of Unity. If listened for, and attuned to, the practice becomes quite simply the natural expression of Being. As in meditation, or yoga, or prayer, or any other practice, there is simply the coming (time and again) to a surrendering into the subtle language of Life that rides within (and without), before (and after) the practice. It is always here, as the very essence of our one, true Being. When we find this, we are Free.

CATCHING YOURSELF:

The trick is not to grab or grasp any of these guiding lights and hold on to them like a badge of entrance, thus giving them more importance than they have. When this happens, you've just been tricked again. As soon as something is grasped too tightly, it is a sure sign that the mind is trying to *use it* to stave off fear, and the threat of non-being. When this is really what is happening, you will hear yourself saying something like, *"Oh, this is it. This is the answer I've been seeking. This is my true direction!"* And you will likely feel a kind of inner relief, like *"Ah, this feels safe, this feels like the answer to all my problems, this is it!—ah, sweet relief (sigh)."*

BUZT! *"Who ya gonna call?..."* Mind-Busters!

Whenever you hear yourself saying (or feel yourself feeling) something like the above, consider the possibility that it's probably another clever mind-trick to keep you inside the globe of self-identity. It's like putting *Fixall*™ over the crack that opened to your remembering. When it is true wisdom (and not a trick), there is no identification or need to grasp anything. An insight or a direction is simply seen and naturally expressed without effort or identification with it. That's the chief distinguishing difference.

WHEN THE GOING REALLY GETS TOUGH:

I am aware as I am writing this section that the wish to offer practical suggestions (as I have above) could give a feeling of simply gathering one's supplies for a little outing in the woods. As practical suggestions that have been helpful in my own journey, I trust they serve you in good stead. Still, I want to say something more here.

I want to put a small light on the really destitute times of emptiness, numbness, confusion, and despair. They are real places you must encounter in yourself if you allow the process to unfold into Remembering, that is, if you can withstand the temptation to apply *Fixall*™ to each crack as you are opened to life, and the Fullness of Being. Perhaps we can only talk around these places. Perhaps the best I can offer are those few pages from my journal at those times in which I was deeply immersed in despair and numbness. But I tell you, it can drag on and on. And at some point in the journey there is no coming back until what was started, is made complete.

At some point, you will have no more choice but to surrender into however this process goes for you. I'm speaking most directly about the inevitable time of falling into the dark night of the soul. It is inevitable, this experience; it occurs spontaneously at the apex of the power shift. It occurs at the moment that the ego-identity sees that it must get down from the throne; when the illusion of its sovereignty is dispelled. It is one terrible experience of loss, sadness, and nothingness. This point marks the place of no returning.

Once the fall has started, *and if* your intent for awakening is true and strong, you must surrender into wherever the process of undoing takes you. How long it takes is no longer in your control. What is asked of you is no longer under your command. You see, the "you" in charge, has changed from the ego-identity "you", to your Original Source. The *ego-king* has stepped down. He is no longer able to take the command; he has been sacrificed to "something more", and the *self-identified you* has no choice but to live it. A fundamental change in power has taken place. You have stepped into Life, only it feels like death because, to the old regime, in a way, it is.

I hope I have well expressed through the sharing of my own experience in the second part of this book, this apex of despair when the power has just shifted from being identified with ego-self to being reestablished in Soul-Source. At some point after the vertigo had ceased to be the problem, it was no longer the case that I was *physically unable* to become engaged in life (i.e., resume my research business, or create art, or socialize with friends). Rather, it was that I had been called by a deeper force awakening in me, *not to* engage in these activities. I was held to non-doing for over a year, with no say at all as to when (or if!) it would ever change or abate. If I had forced it to abate through a rationalized need to get a job, or contribute to society, or because I prematurely grabbed at dream analysis or any other external activity as my savior, my "IT", then I would have been declaring the journey off and the intent for Soul, null and void. This is often a very difficult part of the journey to recognize, to understand, and to accept.

At some point along the path, all I can say is, prematurely ending the process of undoing is no longer an option. When the "I" that wants to "call it off" has been dethroned by that which is your Original Nature, it is simply no longer in a position of stature to make that call.

I was held in a state of wandering non-doing month after month, until my surrender was complete. And you, in your Journey of Awakening will be held (in whatever ways suit your evolution and intent) until your surrender, too, is complete. Not in the same way, not with the same story as mine, but held by the force of your living prayer—by your Soul's intent—until your surrender is complete in whatever way is *complete* for your soul at this time.[1] The good news is, you will never be taken further than your soul intends. You will only come to the place of your living prayer. But it won't feel like that. The fall and the surrender are still terrible, and hard.

In my experience, it is the gentle diligence of being consciously aware and attuned to the living prayer of continual awakening that is the primary calling in this process of *undoing*. To do so requires steadfastness in faith against a terrible backdrop of hopelessness, despair, loss, and nothingness. The experience of staying consciously aware and focused on the living prayer of awakening is a kind of training of the inner ear to attune to a new language, the language of Unity.

And one day, when the noise of despair has stopped and the surrender is complete, you will find yourself very simply no longer on a quest, but rather, embraced in the *simple ordinariness* of Living in the Fullness of *who you really are*. And surprise of surprises: from this place of remembering do all of your unique individual talents and gifts reawaken too! These parts of you thought sacrificed,

---

1.   *I believe awakening is a continual process of evolution and unfolding, and not a one-time event (as I have said throughout this writing). Still, each new moment of re-awakening is most probably met in an experience of death by that which held identity prior to the awakening. As in all of nature, there is the cycle of birth, destruction, death, re-creation…*

stand here in the Re-membering, to become expressed and shared within an open fullness of non-attachment and freedom that is Love in service to Life.

LAST WORD ON EGO AND AWAKENING:

One more point in this process must be spoken as clearly as I can make it (returning once more to paradox, and the discovery in quantum physics of the observer effect on recognizing natural phenomenon as *particle* or *wave*). There can be (and often is) in the Journey of Remembering, one or more fundamental experiences of awakening, true moments, where the shift in one's source of identification from the self-created ego to the Soul (or unity-Consciousness), occurs. This moment of shift is the *particle* point of view, but there is also a more contiguous observation of the *wave* when observed from a different stance. This "particle point of view" is felt as the "awakening experience" some call becoming enlightened, born again, and Self-Realized.

For a very few people, this reformation of the seat of power from ego-identity to Living Presence, appears to occur spontaneously through a movement of Grace (and they call this dramatic experience, becoming spontaneously realized or enlightened). I think it is too potentially misleading, and therefore dangerous to look at enlightenment in this way. It pulls in the drama of our ego-identity: *"Was my enlightenment as big as yours? Is this really it?" Mine didn't come with a blue light, did yours?" (asked hesitantly).* And there we are again, objectifying something that is a living *movement* of conscious awareness, not an isolated *thing*. Once that objectifying starts, we're back on slippery footing indeed.

In fact, I have a current (as yet untested theory as far as I am aware) that by and large, the male gender is more prone toward seeking the *"aha"* experiences of radical awakening, and the female gender more likely to experience many subtler and continual experiences of fundamental insight leading to awakening. (Can't help myself: is there a multiple orgasm parallel here?) Men by their natures (maybe even by their bio-chemistry) seem to require the "big bang" of things; woman by theirs seem to do better with a gentler subtlety. I think this is one of the reasons that most of the world avatars and spiritual gurus have tended to be men. Their approach is simply bigger and more obvious.

An unfortunate and misleading result of this emphasis in our culture for the sensational, as well as the high preponderance of male spiritual teachers and lineages, is that it has made us look to, and expect, "big bang" awakening experiences instead of recognizing that this fundamental process can, and often is (maybe even most often) at play in each of our lives all the time, in very incremental, unobvious ways; ways that don't go *"BANG!"*

I believe our appetites for the sensational, the big, the monumental, are a serious hindrance in this ongoing process of awakening awareness. We, as a result of these appetites, and as a result of the tendency to get the "big bang" theory of enlightenment in disproportion to the more subtle ways of unfolding, are being influenced to look in the wrong ways for the wrong things. We want *big*. We want *bang*. Otherwise it "ain't real". Little of life's inner workings bear this out.

Perhaps most directly to the point, this awakening experience (however it occurs, through a "big bang" or through incremental shifts) *does not* mean that ego no longer exists. It does. The ego self will continue to function, and it will continue to catch you in moments of ego-identification. The same antics you saw and transcended in a moment of awakening, will continue to run through your stream of consciousness. Don't get fooled. You can absolutely descend back into the ego-universe. And you will. Know that you will, and you can catch yourself more quickly by the sensitization of an awareness that is grounded in your deeper Being. Believe you've transcended, and you are surely doomed to endless self-delusion. We're never fully free of ego-identification because we still contain form, and we still function as a human being with its own unique set of gifts, personality, temperament, or as author/philosopher Ken Wilber puts it: from within our unique "spectrum of consciousness".

We can only live within a gentling awareness and acceptance of this dynamic interplay between ego-identity and Unity-Consciousness. This is what I meant when I said in Chapter eight that "the journey ends at the doorstep of each present moment and how we live it." (The continual living of renewed Remembering out of forgetting, is "riding the wave" of conscious evolution.) The journey is never over in the awakening experience. It has only leapt (like an excited electron) to a new playing field and depth of awareness. *Here, now,* is the next region of evolution and conscious unfoldment in an infinite tide of ever-evolving Consciousness.

12

Telling Your Story

✦

(Emergence of Soul)

CLAIM YOUR STORY:

In a delightful book *Soul Prints*, which offers many parables and stories based on the Kabalistic Jewish tradition of the mystic's journey of awakening, author Rabbi Marc Gafni suggests that we've only just now reached a point in human evolution where we begin to see that the universal stories of religious avatars, prophets, and sages, are to be told in our own individual stories of coming to know ourselves in God, and God in ourselves. I believe he is right.

While the age-old sacred texts and mythic stories that tell of the path *to God* offer invaluable guides to these universal truths, I believe that we've come to a point in the evolution of consciousness where these stories need to be grounded within the conscious storytelling of our own living experience. I believe we are each called to become a voice for telling the Universal Story within each unique spectrum of our individual lives.

There is something fundamentally prayerful and powerful in telling our stories of remembering. And this "telling" takes many different forms: it is in the attention we give to our homes, in the quality of our parenting, the care we give to business relations, by our words and by our deeds. We tell our stories through the quality of awareness that we bring to life in each moment. It is in this quality of presence to Life that Soul is consciously reclaimed and the Sacred Story is told. And in this claiming presence, we are automatically redeemed into the *a priori* wholeness that has been ever-present and all around us from the very beginning.

◆   ◆   ◆

How shall we reflect our stories of the journey home? How do we find the thread of this sacred tale? We find those threads in the moments when we stay connected; those times we feel most alive and present for life, *as it is*. Each time that we speak with awareness, dance with awareness, cook with awareness, make love with awareness, cry with awareness, give with awareness, we claim our redemption in the fullness of our Being.

There is a story line (a subtext in a way) that runs through each of our entire lives (if we really look for that thread). You can discover this thread for yourself by looking back over the inner intent of your life (and finding what I call your "Original Living Prayer"). Once it is glimpsed, even if it is only ever so barely sensed as a deep yearning, you will have found the thread calling you to remember your Original Wholeness.

This is so for all of us. There is an ever-patient calling. And whether it is this year or five lifetimes from now, the voice of our Original Nature will bring each of us into Her embrace. Even when we're (seemingly) off the path, somewhere deep down, we're being called to Remember.

Isn't it ironic? To come to the Story of Remembering we have to give up all our little and big stories about "who we think we are"; we have to give up the attachments to our ego-identities. In the giving up of these stories, we come to remember the Fullness *of who we really are*. And here in that Fullness we find, to our surprise, that the uniqueness of our life stories—that which makes us each an unique spectrum of Consciousness ever unfolding—is celebrated and honored within the One Storytelling. Here we find ourselves redeemed in a Fullness of Being that embraces, and delights too, in our full individuality and uniqueness. No thing is lost in the Remembering. Everything is united into All.

I pray that the telling of my story resonates in you; that it helps you to see and to honor the magnificent beauty, uniqueness, and subtlety of your own. This is the One Story we are each called to remember. It is the Sacred Journey we are all called to make.

I pray that you come to this: the telling of *who you really are*; and by the flame of your storytelling, may another one be ignited. And so, by each story told, will another remember, and thus the Great Dreaming awakes!

A Prayer into
the Dark Night of Soul

For those who take up the Soul's Quest,

I pray that the essence of these words will fall on your path and provide some small thread of remembrance and recognition when the way turns black.

I pray that you can stay diligent—and yet gentle to the process; that you will not quit too soon, but will stop to rest when it becomes too much;

that you will never stop listening for that "still small voice" calling to be set free within an all-encompassing and unfathomable darkness; that you will continue on, even when you feel no hope whatsoever;

that when you feel dry and as if nothing of you is left (when you feel completely numb and empty of any reason or meaning at all) that you will offer up a prayer (even a feeble prayer, one without hope)—and let that one small prayer spill out into the endless Stillness of night.

I tell you this now (though you won't believe me when you are at the doorsteps of despair). The prayer is always heard!

The prayer is heard throughout the entire vast universe, and it ripples to touch an infinity of souls: both those who have and have not yet taken up this great soul's Quest of Remembering.

Of those who have made this journey throughout eons of time: They will hear your prayer and they will cry a million tears for you when you can no longer find reason to shed one.

And of those who have not yet taken this journey: They will hear your prayer and they will know a hero is calling them to the courage to face their own Reclamation of Soul.

And, I pray you will not underestimate the gift you give. This is where the Sacred Heart is released. And (if it is to be), this is how humanity shall be redeemed. Each soul: Each a hero's own journey.

I pray you return, a Hero's homecoming: One who, knowing her True Nature, walks in great beauty, humility, compassion and grace...vibrant in the Fullness of Being.

Reading List

I've always been an avid reader. Below are just a few of the key works that have most profoundly aided my Soul's journey. To each author (including many not listed as well as those yet to be discovered) I offer my gratitude.

Campbell, Peter A. and Edwin M. McMahon; *Bio-Spirituality: Focusing as a Way to Grow.* Chicago: Loyola Press; 2nd edition, 1977.

Chopra, Deepak M.D.; *The Seven Spiritual Laws of Success.* San Rafael: Amber-Allen Publishing; Unabridged edition, 2002.

Douglas-Klotz, Neil; *The Hidden Gospel.* Quest Books, 2001.

Easwaran, Eknath; *Dialogue with Death: The Spiritual Psychology of the Katha Upanishad.* Berkeley: Nilgiri Press, 1981.

Gafni, Marc; *Soul Prints: Your Path to Fulfillment.* New York: Pocket Books, 2001.

Ghose, Sisikumar; *Mystics as a Force for Change.* Weaton: Theosophical Publishing House, 1981.

Harrison, Steven; *Doing Nothing: Coming to the End of the Spiritual Search.* New York: Jeremy P. Tarcher/Putnam, 1998.

Hopes David B.; *A Sense of the Morning: Nature Through New Eyes.* Dodd Mead,1988.

Jaidar, George; *The Soul: An Owners Manual.* New York: Paragon House, 1995.

James, William; *The Varieties of Religious Experience.* Signet Classic, 2003.

Joy, Brugh W.; *Avalanche: Heretical Reflections on the Dark and the Light.* New York: Random House, 1992.

Jung, Carl; (Numerous selected works.)

Katie, Byron and Stephen Mitchell (contributor); *Loving What Is: Four Questions That Can Change Your Life.* Harmony Books; 1st edition, 2002.

Kavenaugh, Phillip, M.D.; *The Magnificent Addiction.* Santa Rosa: Aslan Publishing, 1992.

Krishnamurti, J.; *Think On These Things.* New York: Harper & Row, 1970.

Ladinsky, Daniel; *I Heard God Laughing: Renderings of Hafiz.* Oakland: Mobius Press, 1996.

Merrell-Wolff, Franklin; *Experience and Philosophy: A Personal Record of Transformation and a Discussion of Transcendental Consciousness.* Albany: State University of New York Press, 1994.

Minsky, Marvin L.; *The Society of Mind.* Touchstone Books, 1988.

Mitchell, Stephen; *Tao Te Ching (New English Version).* New York: HarperPerennial,1991.

Moore, Thomas; *Care of the Soul: A Guide for Cultivating Depth and Sacredness in Everyday Life.* Perennial Press; Reprint edition, 1994.

Morrison, Scott; *There is Only Now: A Simple Guide to Spiritual Awakening, Unconditional Love, Liberation, and Transformation.* 21st Century Renaissance Publishing, 1996.

Moss, Richard,M.D.; *The Black Butterfly: An Invitation to Radical Aliveness.* Ten Speed Press, 1987.

Moss, Richard, M.D.; *The Second Miracle: Intimacy, Spirituality and Conscious Relationships.* Celestial Arts, 1995.

Novak, Philip; *The World's Wisdom: Sacred Texts of the World's Wisdom.* Harper SanFrancisco,1995.

Pierrakos, Eva and Judith Saly; *Creating Union: The Pathwork of Relationship.* Del Mar: Pathwork Press, 1993.

Sheinkin, David; *Path of the Kabbalah.* St Paul: Paragon House Publishers, 1986.

Speeth, Kathleen Riordan; *The Gurdjieff Work.* New York: Jeremy P. Tarcher/ Perigee, 1989

Talbot, Michael; *Holographic Universe.* Perennial Press, 1992.

Taylor, Jeremy; *Dream Work: Techniques for Discovering the Creative Power in Dreams.* Ramsey: Paulist Press, 1983.

Thurston, Mark; *Discovering Your Soul's Purpose.* Edgar Cayce Foundation, 1984

Trungpa, Chogyam; *The Myth of Freedom And Way of Meditation.* Shambhala Publications, 2002.

Welwood, John; *Toward a Psychology of Awakening: Buddhism, Psychotherapy, and the Path of Personal and Spiritual Transformation.* Boston: Shambhala Publications, 2000.

Wilber, Ken; *The Spectrum of Consciousness.* Quest Books, 1993.

Zukav, Gary; *Seat of the Soul.* Fireside; Reprint edition, 1990.

Zukav, Gary; *The Dancing Wu Li Masters: An Overview of the New Physics.* Mass Paperback, 1994.

Acknowledgements

To my mother, Carol Osborne Ackles, who has been my most ardent reader/reviewer/editor, and who, by her living example, has given me an abundant dose of unconditional loving and radiant joy, I give my deepest gratitude and love. Likewise, I am deeply indebted to my husband of the past 13 years, Steve LaRue, who sees deeply, lives gently, and who has gifted and supported me in more ways than can ever be counted or fully known. I also thank the many friends who read the early versions and offered comments, questions, and editorial support for this work, especially Pamela Pride, Isabella Cordero di Montezemolo, and Marguerite Kownslar for their significant contributions, and Julia Taft Whitman ("*ggg*") for keeping me blazing (or, at if not *blazing* exactly, at least on) the trail! I thank Barbara Deal, literary agent, for taking me on as a fist-time author, teaching me the ropes of publishing, and offering me selfless publishing advice; and the professional staff at iUniverse for their unwavering professionalism and impressive service.

And to my friend and mentor Richard Moss, my heart is blessed and honored by your presence in my life and your enthusiastic support of this book.

About the Author

Ronda Ackles LaRue, originally from Skaneate-les, New York (where she spends summers and still considers home), attended school in the sub-urbs outside of Chicago. After high school, Ronda collected an array of colleges as her ver-sion of "traveling around for awhile", attending five undergraduate and four graduate universi-ties, leading to an undergraduate degree in Busi-ness Psychology (*University of Texas at Dallas*), and a Master's of Science degree in Social Psy-chology: Applied Research Methods (*Texas Christian University*). After college, Ronda moved to Los Angeles where she founded, *Info Vision Systems*, a corporate research consulting practice.

In 1990, Ronda left the "LA freeway jam" and moved to her current home in Ojai, California; a beautiful mountainous valley just south of Santa Barbara, noted world-wide as the home of East Indian philosopher J. Krishnamurti, and a vital gathering place for world-renowned artists, poets, spiritualists, scientists, and musicians seeking a simple lifestyle and the collaboration of ideas.

Ronda is regionally known today, for her work as an artist, poet, and soulful facilitator. She offers unique customized retreats to groups and individuals seek-ing spiritual/creative renewal.

Ronda most enjoys cooking for her "Friday dinners", when friends and neigh-bors stop by for sometimes rousing, always unpredictable, evenings filled with boisterous conversation, candlelit dinners, dancing, drumming, or poetry and prayers shared around the outdoor garden fire pit.

For more information about Ronda's other contemplative writings, art works, book orders, workshops, customized retreats or private sessions, please see: www.rondalarue.com

0-595-29158-9